Cambridge
Collections

Urban voices

a collection of writing on city life

Edited by Mike Gould
Series editor: Michael Marland

CAMBRIDGE
UNIVERSITY PRESS

In memory of Michael Marland (1934–2008).

CAMBRIDGE UNIVERSITY PRESS
Cambridge, New York, Melbourne, Madrid, Cape Town, Singapore, São Paulo, Delhi

Cambridge University Press
The Edinburgh Building, Cambridge CB2 8RU, UK

www.cambridge.org
Information on this title: www.cambridge.org/9780521730839

© Cambridge University Press 2009

This publication is in copyright. Subject to statutory exception and to the provisions of relevant collective licensing agreements, no reproduction of any part may take place without the written permission of Cambridge University Press.

Printed in the United Kingdom at the University Press, Cambridge

A catalogue record for this publication is available from the British Library

ISBN 978-0-521-73083-9 paperback

Cover image: Digital Vision
Cover design by Smith
Illustrations by Paul Dickinson

Cambridge University Press has no responsibility for the persistence or accuracy of URLs for external or third-party Internet websites referred to in this publication, and does not guarantee that any content on such websites is, or will remain, accurate or appropriate. Information regarding prices, travel timetables and other factual information given in this work are correct at the time of first printing but Cambridge University Press does not guarantee the accuracy of such information thereafter.

Contents

10 29/4/17

10 7/5/17

General introduction

Urban voices is a collection of stories, poems, plays and non-fiction texts that explore the experiences of people living in cities. What are living conditions like? How does 'city life' compare with living in other environments, such as the countryside? What concerns and worries do people living in cities have? How is life different for the rich and poor? It's a collection that may well link with other studies you do in Humanities – such as Geography, or Citizenship and PSHE – as it focuses on people and how they respond to their environment. However, first and foremost it is a book to be read and enjoyed in English lessons, with a wide range of activities related to the stories the texts tell, the language the writers use, and the themes and issues they explore.

The book is divided into five sections. The first, *Five cities*, takes five cities from different regions of the world and explores life there, both in the present day and the past. What is life like living in one of the largest slums in the world? How did two writers living in the same century (Wordsworth and Blake) come to have such different views about London? How does a modern-day writer create a picture of a city from almost two thousand years ago?

This landscape, these people explores the experience of people who have moved to – or from – cities, and how it has changed their lives and viewpoints. For example, there is a fictional account of a boy who has arrived in a South African city and is fighting to survive on the streets, and a 19th-century dialogue poem between a town girl and a country girl, as well as tales of immigration and departure. How does it feel to return to a place you left many years before? What is it like living or working in a big city after time spent in the countryside? How does it feel to move from a city on one continent to another?

Penthouse and pavement is the title of the next section and explores the contrasts that the texts within it seek to describe, between those who are wealthy enough to live in penthouse apartments and those whose only home is the street or pavement upon which they sleep. The texts show how this is a problem not just for poorer countries around the world, or the UK in years gone past, but a problem of here and now.

Gangs, groups, friends and foes begins with a fictional text about two different groups of people living above and below the streets, and how the 'Throwbacks' stick together to survive against the 'Updwellers'. The texts in this section raise the question: if gangs and groups make people feel secure, why are so many of them involved in conflict? And what makes one group of people oppose another? Is it race, class, money, place – or other things?

Hear me speak provides a chance for those who live in cities – especially those who are oppressed or living in difficult circumstances – to speak or write about their experiences, whether it is trying to explain the Paris riots of 2007 or why a man living by himself in a comfortable city feels isolated and alone. Are cities places that bring us community and friendship, or do they encourage fear, conflict or loneliness?

Each section is arranged so that the more difficult pieces are placed at the end of the section. To support your reading, certain words (these are numbered) in the texts are explained in the footnotes. Ideas for further reading accompany each text. Each section concludes with a range of reading, writing, speaking, listening and drama activities to help you explore and enjoy the authors' ideas, opinions, style, language and techniques.

The text-specific activities pages are divided into the following activity types: *Before you read* (pre-reading stimulation activities), *What's it about?* (comprehension-style questions) and *Thinking about the text* (activities that move beyond the text itself). At the very end of each section, a series of *Compare and contrast* activities provides opportunities to compare two or more texts.

I hope you enjoy reading and exploring the range of texts here. There is a wide variety, including stories, poems, articles, autobiographical writing, drama, articles, and much more. A number of the texts, particularly some of the fictional ones, were written specifically for people of your age, but many weren't. However, the book was put together with you in mind – to stimulate debate, to make you think, to encourage you to explore the lives of people and places beyond your immediate experience, or make you look again at the world around you. I hope it will give you a new perspective on what it is like to live in these strange urban environments we call 'cities' and 'towns', and the challenges and opportunities they bring.

Mike Gould

1 Five cities

The first section of the book presents a range of large cities from different parts of the world, both in fictional and non-fiction texts. You will read about people living in dreadful poverty in present-day Mumbai, as well as the glittering, high-tech world of Tokyo in Graham Marks's novel. Bill Bryson describes two contrasting sides of Philadelphia, and we visit the richness of the Roman Empire in Robert Harris's *Pompeii*. Finally, two contrasting views are presented of London in Blake's and Wordsworth's poems.

Activities

1   Think about poems, stories or novels you have read in which cities are the main settings. Make brief notes about what impressions are given of them: are the cities presented as pleasant, enjoyable places to live, or as cruel, poor or unwelcoming – or perhaps a mix of both?

2   Now think about television programmes, films or plays that are set in cities. Discuss them in pairs or small groups. How important are these cities to the story and to the characters' lives?

3   The texts in this section deal with five cities: Mumbai (once called Bombay) in India; Tokyo; the ancient Roman city of Pompeii; Philadelphia in the United States; and London from over a hundred years ago. In small groups, take it in turns to choose one of these places (which you shouldn't have visited), and discuss why you would like to go there and what you would expect it to be like.

Tokyo

by Graham Marks

> In this extract from the novel by Graham Marks, Adam is searching
> for his sister Charlie, who has disappeared in mysterious circum-
> stances while travelling with a friend. In the section you are about
> to read, Adam has spent the night in a special tube-like room which
> he only has space to lie down in.

Adam woke up with a start, lying still in the semi-darkness,
trying to work out where the hell he was. Something, a noise,
must've dragged him out of a deep, deep sleep because nothing in his head seemed to be working very efficiently. He
rolled over on to his back and his elbow banged on to something hard; he touched it: plastic. Plastic? His eyes finally
adjusted to the light level and he remembered where he was.
Tokyo. In a box. He pressed the 'light' button on his watch
and saw it was 9:30, but whether that was a.m. or p.m. he had-
n't the slightest idea.

Toky-oh-my-God . . . it was all Adam could think as he stood in
the street, looking at the night-time version of Asakusa going
on around him. Then he gazed up at the sky, expecting stars,
but in a different pattern to the one he'd see at home.

Nothing, just black. No stars. Neon[1] all the way.

A whole world of neon. Every colour of the rainbow, except
the subtle ones. Flashing on and off, rising and falling like elec-
tronic, coloured rain . . . pictures, symbols, graphics, all glowing
in the night. And there, among the random, alien light-sprawl,
the occasional English words, just to add to the confusion.

*PARODY MARKET . . . MY WAY . . . FREE . . . GENIUS AMUSE-
MENT . . .*

---

[1] **neon**   bright white and coloured lights used for advertisements and street
  lighting

Meaningless words trying to make themselves heard amongst the indecipherable visual noise² and the cars and the people and the piped music³ and the conversations. Was everyone here talking to someone else on a mobile phone? It certainly looked that way, with those not talking deeply involved in texting. Adam wondered what a Japanese text message looked like. Very different. Like now. Nothing looked the same as it had during the day and Adam suddenly felt completely disoriented.

'Jeez . . . ' What had he done, coming here? How was he ever going to have a chance of finding Charlie in this madhouse – what had he been thinking? He couldn't work out how come it had ever seemed like a good idea, how come Suzy hadn't told him to get real. But she hadn't, he was here and he knew he had to deal with it. Completely his responsibility. As the world flowed around him, it occurred to Adam that he had two

---

²**indecipherable visual noise**   a muddle of lights that makes them unreadable
³**piped music**   recorded and amplified music

choices: go home, the first chance he had, or have a go at doing what he'd come here for.

If he didn't actually make a move, *do* something, he felt like he'd still be standing on this bit of pavement, dithering, when the sun came up. He'd already figured out that the tube map in the guidebook was much harder to make sense of than the one included in the fold-out city map he'd bought; standing in a pool of streetlight he took another look, seeing that he was actually just eleven stops from Roppongi. It could not be that difficult a journey to do, and he'd at least be able to start his search for the Bar Belle and feel he hadn't wasted the whole of his first day in Tokyo.

Underground there was a new world, a bright, clean environment which, considering the neon mayhem going on above it, was astonishingly free of excessive advertising. Working out how to buy a ticket, though, had proved to be no easy job – even after he'd found the button which changed the Japanese characters on the text screen into English. Luckily someone who turned out to understand more English than they actually spoke spotted him standing, dazed and confused, in front of a bank of ticket machines, and between them they'd managed to buy a ticket that Adam hoped would get him to Roppongi and back again.

After the frustrating ticket-buying experience, the journey turned out to be a breeze, just a question of paying attention and following instructions and numbers, of going from A18 to E23, through colour-coded tunnels and on south-bound trains. Simple.

Exiting Roppongi station Adam found himself back in Neon City and at what appeared to be a major crossroads. There was an elevated expressway[4] running above one of the streets which had a sign on it in English letting him know he was now in 'High Touch Town', whatever that actually meant. From what the guidebook said, it probably meant what it sounded like. And somewhere here there was a place called the

---

[4]**elevated expressway**   a motorway raised above street level

Bar Belle, where Alice and Charlie had been working, and where Alice had last seen Charlie walking out with a customer.

As he had no idea where the girls' apartment was he'd *got* to find the bar. It was the only place to start, the only place he'd be able to hook up with Alice and find out for himself exactly what was going on. Get to talk to Alice's boyfriend, Steve, see what he had to say.

The only problem was he had absolutely no idea where in Roppongi - no small area - to find the Bar Belle. Before leaving England he'd looked it up on the Net, having discovered that a lot of the bars had their own websites, but found nothing. Was it too small? Too scuzzy?[5] Just not bothered? He'd have to find it first to know, but how? Then, above the roar of the traffic, he heard a badly amplified voice calling out, something about beer and girls and music. Now he looked he could see that there were quite a few people, types he recognised from Soho and Brixton, touting[6] various clubs and bars; one of them was using a cardboard megaphone. Most of them were black and one of them might know something. Whether they'd tell him was another matter entirely.

Adam chose the least threatening-looking of the guys and hoped you could judge this particular book by its cover. He approached, friendly, smiling. 'Speak English, man?'

'Chor, wa'choo wan? Nice girl? Cheap booze? We got de bes in town!' All teeth and big smiles, the man thrust a coloured flyer at Adam. 'Jus roun da corner, man, two minutes - you go?'

Adam looked at the piece of paper in his hand: Club Exit. 'No, I'm looking for this place called the Bar Belle, you heard of it?'

'Chor I hear . . . terrible place, man, you wan class? You go Exit, man. Lemme take you roun . . .'

'I need to find the Bar Belle, I'm meeting a friend there and I lost the address.'

'Piece a dirt place, man.'

---

[5]**scuzzy**   dirty, unpleasant
[6]**touting**   pestering people to become customers

Adam dug into his jeans pocket and brought out one of the
¥1,000 notes[7] he'd stuffed in there after buying his subway
ticket. 'I really don't care . . .'

The man reached out to take it and Adam moved his hand
back. 'OK, right . . . OK, man, see, you go cross da street, you
take secon right, you fine it up a few floor, five or six, I don
'member zackly. Look for da sign, man.'

'Thanks.' Adam handed over the note.

It wasn't there. Across the street, second on the right, was a narrow alleyway which restaurants backed on to. It was full of
industrial-sized wheelie bins, it smelt of cooking and food and
the remains of cleared plates that had sat out in the heat for too
long. There was no Bar Belle, not at ground level or five or six
floors up, no matter how far down he went . . .

Adam turned to go back up the way he'd come, and
stopped. Silhouetted against the bright lights of the main drag[8]
he saw a figure that seemed to be looking his way, waiting . . .
Had he been set up here? More than likely. He looked behind
him, back down into the gloom of what looked like a dead end;
no point in running down there, then. He cast around in the
shadow on the ground for anything he might be able to use to
defend himself, and saw nothing.

Walking slowly back up the alley Adam thought about trying to fit some coins between his fingers, make iron knuckles,
like he'd seen done in a movie, but he knew he was clutching at
straws now. Best just to go for this head on, wait until the last
minute and make a rush for the street and hope he got past the
guy. He'd be safe out in the crowds. Safer, anyway.

He'd been psyching himself up so much that it was only
when he was just about to start running like hell, possibly
yelling at the top of his voice, that he realised the person was
not only standing with his back to the alley, not looking down

---

[7]**¥1,000 note**   Japanese currency note, one thousand yen
[8]**main drag**   the main street

it at all, he was also much nearer to the street than he'd realised. And, as the man turned to look to his right, Adam could now see he was quite an old guy.

The feeling of panic subsided, replaced by one of embarrassment as he walked past the man and out on to the pavement; how stupid would he have felt, tearing past this total stranger like a madman? Total dimwit stupid.

Accompanied by an odd sense of anticlimax, Adam made his way back to the big junction and the subway station. He looked at his watch: a quarter to midnight. he didn't know when the trains stopped running, but he'd better not risk missing the last one by hanging round this place much longer; tomorrow he'd come back again and do it properly this time.

Further reading

Stories in which people disappear provide thrilling, if often sad, subject matter. A novel that is less thriller and more a study of human despair, is Ian McEwan's *The Child in Time* (Bloomsbury, 1987) which is about the disappearance of a child from a supermarket and the consequent effect on the parents.

India: A Million Mutinies Now

by V. S. Naipaul

> The book from which this extract comes describes the visit of the author to the country in the title. In this extract, he has asked a friend, Papu, to show him the huge slum area of Mumbai called 'Dharavi' which is very close to the wealthier area in which Papu lives.

I thought that Papu had given up the idea of the visit to the great slum of Dharavi. But his spirits had revived in the sitting room of his flat, and after our tea he took me to a back room, to show me the view. The slum was closer than I thought. It lay just beyond the railway tracks that ran at the back of the street on which Papu's block stood. Papu's middle-class area, so established-looking when one came to the street, was contained in a narrow strip between the area of the quarters[1] and the area of the great slum.

He said, of the slum, 'You wouldn't be able to stand the stink.'

A little later, with the determination and suddenness with which people go out into bad weather, he said we should be going.

We set out on foot. The slum was only a short walk away. We began to cross the busy, dusty bridge over the railway lines. The afternoon traffic was hectic. We had barely got down the hump of the railway bridge, when Papu, losing a little of his resolution, said we should take a taxi.

To stress the extent of the slum, he said, 'Look. No tall buildings from here to there.' It was a good way of taking it in. Otherwise, moving at road level, one might have missed the extent of the flat ragged plain, bounded by far-off towers.

And then, in no time, we were moving on the margin of the slum, so sudden, so obvious, so overwhelming, it was as though

---

[1] **quarters**   a section of the city where more formal buildings are found

it was something staged, something on a film set, with people acting out their roles as slum dwellers: back-to-back and side-to-side shacks and shelters, a general impression of blackness and greyness and mud, narrow ragged lanes curving out of view; then a side of the main road dug up; then black mud, with men and women and children defecating on the edge of a black lake, swamp and sewage, with a hellish oily iridescence.[2]

The stench was barely supportable; but it had to be endured. The taxi came to a halt in a traffic jam. The jam was caused by a line of loaded trucks on the other side of the road. The slum of Dharavi was also an industrial area of sorts, with many unauthorized businesses, leather works and chemical works among them, which wouldn't have been permitted in a better regulated city area.

Petrol and kerosene fumes added to the stench. In this stench, many bare-armed people were at work, doing what I had never seen people doing before: gathering or unpacking cloth waste and cardboard waste, working in a grey-white dust that banked up on the ground like snow and stifled the sounds of hands and feet, working beside the road itself or in small shanties: large-scale rag-picking.[3]

Papu said he hardly passed this way. In the taxi he sat turned away from the slum itself. He faced the other side of the road, where the loaded trucks were idling, and where, in the distance, were the apartment blocks of the middle-class area of Bandra, on the sea.

The traffic moved again. At a certain point Papu said, 'This is the Muslim section. People will tell you that the Muslims here are fundamentalists.[4] But don't you think you could make these people fight for anything you tell them to fight for?'

---

[2]**iridescence**   displaying rainbow-like colours, often seen where water is polluted by oil or chemicals

[3]**rag-picking**   people in slums often make a living by sorting and selling the city's rubbish

[4]**fundamentalists**   people with extreme religious views

The stench of animal skins and excrement and swamp and chemicals and petrol fumes, the dust of cloth waste, the amber mist of truck exhausts, with the afternoon sun slanting through – what a relief it was to leave that behind, and to get out into the other Bombay, the Bombay one knew and had spent so much time getting used to, the Bombay of paved roads and buses and people in lightweight clothes.

It had been hard enough to drive past the area. It was harder to imagine what it was like living there. Yet people lived with the stench and the terrible air, and had careers there. Even lawyers lived there, I was told. Was the smell of excrement only on the periphery, from the iridescent black lake? No; that stench went right through Dharavi. Even more astonishing was to read in a Bombay magazine an article about Papu's suburb of Sion, in which the slum of Dharavi was written about almost as a bohemian[5] feature of the place, something that added spice to humdrum middle-class life. Bombay clearly inoculated[6] its residents in some way.

I had another glimpse of Dharavi some time later, when I was going in a taxi to the domestic airport at Santa Cruz. The taxi-driver – a Muslim from Hyderabad, full of self-respect, nervous about living in Bombay, fearful of sinking, planning to go back home soon, and in the meantime nervously particular about his car and his clothes – the taxi-driver showed the apartment blocks on one side of the airport road where hutment dwellers had been rehoused. In the other direction he showed the marsh on which Dharavi had grown and, away in the distance, the low black line of the famous slum.

Seen from here, Dharavi looked artificial, unnecessary even in Bombay: allowed to exist because, as people said, it was a vote-bank, a hate-bank, something to be drawn upon by many

---

[5]**bohemian**   a little strange and unconventional, but interesting

[6]**inoculated**   literally means 'treated against disease'; here, the author uses the word to suggest that the inhabitants of the city seem to overlook, or not see, Dharavi's problems

people. All the conflicting currents of Bombay flowed there as well; all the new particularities were heightened there. And yet people lived there, subject to this extra exploitation, because in Bombay, once you had a place to stay, you could make money.

Further reading

If you found this text interesting, you may wish to read more of the book from which it came, V. S. Naipaul's *India: A Million Mutinies Now* (Heinemann, 1990). Naipaul is a well-known novelist and has written about the lives of Indian people elsewhere, for example in *A Bend in the River* (Random House, 1979) which is set in an unnamed African city. You may also like to read *Broken Glass* by Sally Grindley (Bloomsbury, 2008), author of *Spilled Water* in section 2, which tells the story of two Indian children who end up on the streets, after running away from their violent father.

Pompeii

by Robert Harris

The novel *Pompeii* tells the story of the events that lead up to the destruction of a Roman city by the volcano Vesuvius in AD 79. The story is told through the eyes of Attilius, a young engineer who has just been made responsible for the water supply to the cities in the Bay of Naples. In this extract, he is arriving in Pompeii for the first time, in order to discover why the water supply has failed in other towns nearby. He is accompanied by his assistant, an older man, Corax.

She came into view slowly from behind a headland, and she was not at all what the engineer had expected – no sprawling resort like Baiae or Neapolis, strung out along the coastline of the bay, but a fortress-city, built to withstand a siege, set back a quarter of a mile from the sea, on higher ground, her port spread out beneath her.

It was only as they drew closer that Attilius saw that her walls were no longer continuous – that the long years of the Roman peace had persuaded the city fathers to drop their guard. Houses had been allowed to emerge above the ramparts, and to spill, in widening, palm-shaded terraces, down towards the docks. Dominating the line of flat roofs was a temple, looking out to sea. Gleaming marble pillars were surmounted by what at first appeared to be a frieze of ebony figures. But the frieze, he realised, was alive. Craftsmen, almost naked and blackened by the sun, were moving back and forth against the white stone – working, even though it was a public holiday. The ring of chisels on stone and the rasp of saws carried clear in the warm air.

Activity everywhere. People walking along the top of the wall and working in the gardens that looked out to sea. People swarming along the road in front of the town – on foot, on horseback, in chariots and on the backs of wagons – throwing up a haze of dust and clogging the steep paths that led up from the port to the two big city gates. As the *Minerva* turned in to the narrow entrance of the harbour the din of the crowd grew louder – a holiday crowd, by the look of it, coming into town from the countryside to celebrate the festival of Vulcan.[1] Attilius scanned the dockside for fountains but could see none.

The men were all silent, standing in line, each with his own thoughts.

He turned to Corax. 'Where does the water come into the town?'

'On the other side of the city,' said Corax, staring intently at the town. 'Beside the Vesuvius Gate. *If* – ' he gave heavy emphasis to the word ' – it's still flowing.'

That would be a joke, thought Attilius, if it turned out the water was not running after all and he had brought them all this way merely on the word of some old fool of an augur.[2]

'Who works there?'

'Just some town slave. You won't find him much help.'

'Why not?'

Corax grinned and shook his head. He would not say. A private joke.

'All right. Then the Vesuvius Gate is where we'll start from.' Attilius clapped his hands. 'Come on, lads. You've seen a town before. The cruise is over.'

They were inside the harbour now. Warehouses and cranes crowded against the water's edge. Beyond them was a river – the Sarnus, according to Attilius's map – choked with barges waiting to be unloaded. Torquatus, shouting orders, strode down the length of the ship. The drumbeats[3] slowed and ceased. The oars were shipped. The helmsman turned the rudder slightly and they glided alongside the wharf at walking-pace, no more than a foot of clear water between the deck and the quay. Two groups of sailors carrying mooring cables jumped ashore and

---

[1] **Vulcan**   the Roman god of fire
[2] **augur**   someone who foresees events
[3] **drumbeats**   drums were used to beat out the rhythm for Roman oarsmen (who were usually slaves), driving the boat forward

wound them quickly around the stone posts. A moment later the ropes snapped taut and, with a jerk that almost knocked Attilius off his feet, the *Minerva* came to rest.

He saw it as he was recovering his balance. A big, plain stone plinth with a head of Neptune gushing water from his mouth into a bowl that was shaped like an oyster-shell, and the bowl *overflowing* – this was what he would never forget – cascading down to rinse the cobbles, and wash, unregarded, into the sea. Nobody was queuing to drink. Nobody was paying it any attention. Why should they? It was just an ordinary miracle. He vaulted over the low side of the warship and swayed towards it, feeling the strange solidity of the ground after the voyage across the bay. He dropped his sack and put his hands into the clear arc of water, cupped them, raised them to his lips. It tasted sweet and pure and he almost laughed aloud with pleasure and relief, then plunged his head beneath the pipe, and let the water run everywhere – into his mouth and nostrils, his ears, down the back of his neck – heedless of the people staring at him as if he had gone insane.

Hora quarta
[09:48 hours]

Isotope studies[4] of Neapolitan volcanic magma show signs of significant mixing with the surrounding rock, suggesting that the reservoir isn't one continuous molten body. Instead, the reservoir might look more like a sponge, with the magma[5] seeping through numerous fractures in the rock. The massive magma layer may feed into several smaller reservoirs that are closer to the surface and too small to identify with seismic techniques[6] . . .

American Association for the Advancement of Science,
news bulletin, 'Massive Magma Layer feeds
Mt. Vesuvius', November 16, 2001

---

[4]**isotope studies**   scientific measuring which enables students, among other things, to find out how old things are and where they came from
[5]**magma**   molten rock from below the Earth's surface
[6]**seismic techniques**   means of measuring movements in the Earth's crust

A man could buy anything he needed in the harbour of Pompeii.
Indian parrots, Nubian slaves, nitrum salt from the pools near
Cairo, Chinese cinnamon, African monkeys, Oriental slave-girls
famed for their sexual tricks . . . Horses were as easy to come by
as flies. Half a dozen dealers hung around outside the customs
shed. The nearest sat on a stool beneath a crudely drawn sign of
the winged Pegasus, bearing the slogan 'Baculus: Horses Swift
Enough for the Gods'.

'I need five,' Attilius told the dealer. 'And none of your
clapped-out nags. I want good, strong beasts, capable of working all day. And I need them now.'

'That's no problem, citizen.' Baculus was a small, bald man,
with the brick-red face and glassy eyes of a heavy drinker. He
wore an iron ring too large for his finger, which he twisted nervously, round and round. 'Nothing's a problem in Pompeii,
provided you've the money. Mind you, I'll require a deposit.
One of my horses was stolen the other week.'

'And I also want oxen. Two teams and two wagons.'

'On a public holiday?' He clicked his tongue. 'That, I think, will take longer.'

'How long?'

'Let me see.' Baculus squinted at the sun. The more difficult he made it sound, the more he could charge. 'Two hours. Maybe three.'

'Agreed.'

They haggled over the price, the dealer demanding an outrageous sum which Attilius immediately divided by ten. Even so, when eventually they shook hands, he was sure he had been swindled and it irritated him, as any kind of waste always did. But he had no time to seek out a better bargain. He told the dealer to bring round four of the horses immediately to the Vesuvius Gate and then pushed his way back through the traders towards the *Minerva*.

By now the crew had been allowed up on deck. Most had peeled off their sodden tunics and the stench of sweat from the sprawled bodies was strong enough to compete with the stink of the nearby fish-sauce factory, where liquefying offal[7] was decomposing in vats in the sunshine. Corvinus and Becco were picking their way between the oarsmen, carrying the tools, throwing them over the side to Musa and Polites. Corax stood with his back to the boat, peering towards the town, occasionally rising on tiptoe to see over the heads of the crowd.

He noticed Attilius and stopped. 'So the water runs,' he said, and folded his arms. There was something almost heroic about his stubbornness, his unwillingness to concede he had been wrong. It was then that Attilius knew, beyond question, that once all this was over he would have to get rid of him.

'Yes, she runs,' he agreed. He waved to the others to stop what they were doing and to gather round. It was agreed that they would leave Polites to finish the unloading and to guard the tools on the dockside; Attilius would send word to him

---

[7]**offal**   waste material

about where to meet up later. Then the remaining five set off towards the nearest gate, Corax trailing behind, and whenever Attilius looked back it seemed that he was searching for someone, his head craning from side to side.

The engineer led them up the ramp from the harbour towards the city wall, beneath the half-finished temple of Venus and into the dark tunnel of the gate. A customs official gave them a cursory glance to check they were not carrying anything they might sell, then nodded them into the town.

The street beyond the gate was not as steep as the ramp outside, or as slippery, but it was narrower, so that they were almost crushed by the weight of bodies surging into Pompeii. Attilius found himself borne along past shops and another big temple – this one dedicated to Apollo – and into the blinding open space and swarming activity of the forum.

It was imposing for a provincial town: basilica, covered market, more temples, a public library – all brilliantly coloured and shimmering in the sunlight; three or four dozen statues of emperors and local worthies high up on their pedestals. Not all of it was finished. A webwork of wooden scaffolding covered some of the large buildings. The high walls acted to trap the noise of the crowd and reflect it back at them – the flutes and drums of the buskers[8], the cries of the beggars and hawkers,[9] the sizzle of cooking food. Fruit-sellers were offering green figs and pink slices of melon. Wine merchants crouched beside rows of red amphorae[10] propped in nests of yellow straw. At the foot of a nearby statue a snake-charmer sat cross-legged, playing a pipe, a grey serpent rising groggily from the mat in front of him, another draped round his neck. Small pieces of fish were frying on an open range. Slaves, bowed under the weight of bundles of wood, were hurrying in relays to pile them on to the big bonfire

---

[8]**buskers**   street musicians
[9]**hawkers**   street salesmen
[10]**amphorae**   Roman containers for liquid, with two handles and a narrow neck

being built in the centre of the forum for the evening sacrifice to Vulcan. A barber advertised himself as an expert in pulling teeth and had a foot-high pile of grey and black stumps to prove it.

The engineer took off his hat and wiped his forehead. Already there was something about the place he did not much like. A hustler's[11] town, he thought. Full of people on the make. She would welcome a visitor for exactly as long as it took to fleece him.

Further reading

If you'd like to read more by Robert Harris, try *Fatherland* (Random House, 1992). This mixes a great story with historical insight, imagining what would have happened if Hitler and Germany had not lost World War II and nobody had found out about the Holocaust.

---

[11]**hustler**   dishonest person

The Lost Continent

by Bill Bryson

In this extract the author is travelling around America to try to get a sense of what the country he was born in is really like. Here, he visits Philadelphia, and accidentally discovers a part of the city he would have preferred to miss.

When I was a child, Philadelphia was the third biggest city in America. What I remembered of it was driving through endless miles of ghettos,[1] one battered block after another, on a hot July Sunday, with black children playing in the spray of fire hydrants and older people lounging around on the street corners or sitting on the front stoops. It was the poorest place I had ever seen. Trash lay in the gutters and doorways, and whole buildings were derelict. It was like a foreign country, like Haiti or Panama. My dad whistled tunelessly through his teeth the whole time, as he always did when he was uneasy, and told us to keep the windows rolled up even though it was boiling in the car. At stop lights people would stare stonily at us and Dad would whistle in double time and drum the steering wheel with his fingers and smile apologetically at anyone who looked at him, as if to say, 'Sorry, we're from out of state.'

Things have changed now, naturally. Philadelphia is no longer the third biggest city in America. Los Angeles pushed it into fourth place in the 1960s, and now there are freeways to whisk you into the heart of town without soiling your tyres in the ghettos. Even so, I managed a brief, inadvertent visit to one of the poorer neighbourhoods when I wandered off the freeway in search of a gas station. Before I could do anything about it, I found myself sucked into a vortex[2] of one-way streets that carried me into the most squalid and dangerous-looking

---

[1]**ghettos**   parts of a city each occupied by a minority group
[2]**vortex**   whirlwind

neighbourhood I had ever seen. It may have been, for all I know, the very ghetto we passed through all those years before – the brownstone[3] buildings looked much the same – but it was many times worse than the one I remembered. The ghetto of my childhood, for all its poorness, had the air of a street carnival. People wore colourful clothes and seemed to be having a good time. This place was just bleak and dangerous, like a war zone. Abandoned cars, old refrigerators, burnt-out sofas littered every vacant lot. Garbage cans looked as if they had been thrown to the street from the roof-tops. There were no gas stations – I wouldn't have stopped anyway, not in a place like this, not for a million dollars – and most of the storefronts were boarded with plywood. Every standing object had been spray-painted with graffiti. There were still a few young people on the stoops and corners, but they looked listless and cold – it was a chilly day – and they seemed not to notice me. Thank God. This was a neighbourhood where clearly you could be murdered for a pack of cigarettes – a fact that was not lost on me as I searched nervously for a way back onto the freeway. By the time I found it, I wasn't whistling through my teeth so much as singing through my sphincter.

It really was the most uncomfortable experience I had had in many years. God, what it must be like to live there and to walk those streets daily. Do you know that if you are a black man in urban America you now stand a one in nineteen chance of being murdered? In World War II, the odds of being killed were one in fifty. In New York City there is one murder every four hours. Murder there has become the most common cause of death for people under thirty-five – and yet New York isn't even the most murderous city in America. At least eight other cities have a higher murder rate. In Los Angeles there are more murders each year on schoolgrounds alone than there are in the whole of London. So perhaps it is little wonder that people in

---

[3]**brownstone**   buildings made of red-brown sandstone, generally among the older buildings in US cities

American cities take violence as routine. I don't know how they do it.

On my way to Des Moines to start this trip, I passed through O'Hare Airport in Chicago where I ran into a friend who worked for the *St Louis Post Dispatch*. He told me he had been working extra hard lately because of something that had happened to his boss. The boss had been driving home from work late one Saturday night when he had stopped at some traffic lights. As he waited for the lights to change, the passenger door opened and a man with a gun got in. The gunman made the boss drive down to the riverfront, where he shot him in the head and took his money. The boss had been in a coma for three weeks and they weren't sure whether he was going to live.

My friend was telling me this not because it was such an incredible story, but simply by way of elucidating[4] why he was having to work so damned hard lately. As for his boss, his attitude seemed to be that if you forget to lock your car doors when you're driving through St Louis late at night, well, you've got to expect to take a bullet in the head from time to time. It was very odd, his deadpan attitude, but it seems to be more and more the way in America now. It made me feel like a stranger.

I drove downtown[5] and parked near City Hall. On top of the building is a statue of William Penn. It's the main landmark downtown, visible from all around the city, but it was covered in scaffolding. In 1985, after decades of neglect, the city fathers[6] decided to refurbish the statue before it fell down. So they covered it in scaffolding. However, this cost so much that there was no money left to do the repairs. Now, two years later, the scaffolding was still there and not a lick of work had been done. A city engineer had recently announced with a straight face that

---

[4]**elucidating**   explaining
[5]**downtown**   centre of the city
[6]**city fathers**   city authorities, councillors

before long the scaffolding itself would need to be refurbished. This is more or less how Philadelphia works, which is to say, not very well. No other city in America pursues the twin ideals of corruption and incompetence with quite the same enthusiasm. When it comes to asinine[7] administration, Philadelphia is in a league of its own.

Consider: in 1985, a bizarre sect called Move barricaded itself into a tenement house on the west side of town. The police chief and mayor considered the options open to them and decided that the most intelligent use of their resources would be to blow up the house – but of course! – even though they knew there were children inside and it was in the middle of a densely-populated part of the city. So they dropped a bomb on the house from a helicopter. This started a fire that quickly grew out of control and burned down most of the neighbourhood – sixty-one houses in all – and killed eleven people, including all the children in the barricaded home.

When they aren't being incompetent, city officials like to relax with a little corruption. Just as I was driving into town I heard on the radio that a former city councillor had been sentenced to ten years in jail and his aide to eight years for attempted extortion.[8] The judge called it a gross breach of public trust. He should know. Across town a state review board was calling for the dismissal of nine of the judge's colleagues for taking cash gifts from members of the Roofers Union. Two of those judges were already awaiting trial on extortion charges. This sort of thing is routine in Philadelphia. A few months earlier, when a state official named Bud Dwyer was similarly accused of corruption, he called a press conference, pulled out a gun and, as cameras rolled, blew his brains out.

Yet for all its incompetence and criminality, Philadelphia is a likeable place. For one thing, unlike Washington, it feels like a big city. It had skyscrapers and there was steam rising through

---

[7]**asinine**   stupid
[8]**extortion**   obtaining money by force

vents in the sidewalk and on every corner stood a stainless steel hot-dog stand, with a chilly-looking guy in a stocking cap bobbing around behind it. I wandered over to Independence Square – actually it's now called Independence National Historical Park – and looked respectfully at all the historic buildings. The main building is Independence Hall, where the Declaration of Independence was drawn up and the Constitution ratified.[9] When I was first there in 1960, there was a long line stretching out of the building. There still was – in fact, it seemed not to have moved in twenty-seven years. Deep though my respect is for both the Constitution and the Declaration of Independence, I was disinclined to spend my afternoon in such a long and immobile queue. I went instead to the visitors' centre. National park visitors' centres are always the same. They have some displays in glass cases that manage to be both boring and uninformative, a locked auditorium with a board out front saying that the next showing of the free twelve-minute introductory film will be at 4 p.m. (just before 4 p.m. somebody comes and changes it to 10 a.m.), some racks of books and brochures with titles like *Pewter in History* and *Vegetables of Old Philadelphia,* which are too dull even to browse through, much less buy, and a drinking fountain and rest-rooms, which everyone makes use of because there's not much else to do. Every visitor to every national park goes into the visitors' centre, stands around kind of stupidly for a while, then has a pee and a drink of water and wanders back outside. That is what I did now.

From the visitors' centre I ambled along Independence Mall to Franklin Square, which was full of winos, many of whom had the comical idea that I might be prepared to give them twenty-five cents of my own money without their providing any product or service in return. According to my guidebook, Franklin Square had 'lots of interesting things' to see – a museum, a working book bindery, an archaeological exhibit and 'the only post office

---

[9]**ratified**   accepted by mutual agreement

in the United States which does not fly the American flag' (don't ask me why) – but my heart wasn't in it, especially with piteous and unwashed winos tugging at my sleeves all the while, and I fled back to the real world of downtown Philadelphia.

Late in the afternoon, I found my way to the offices of the *Philadelphia Inquirer*, where an old friend from Des Moines, Lucia Herndon, was lifestyle editor. The *Inquirer* offices were like newspaper offices everywhere – grubby, full of junk, littered with coffee-cups in which cigarette butts floated like dead fish in a polluted lake – and Lucia's desk, I was impressed to note, was one of the messiest in the room. This may have accounted in part for her impressive rise at the *Inquirer*.

We drove in my car out to the district of Mt Airy where, conveniently for me – and for her too, come to that – Lucia lived with another old friend of mine from Des Moines, her husband, Hal. All day long I had been wondering, vaguely and inter-mittently, why Hal and Lucia liked Philadelphia so much – they had moved there about a year before – but now I understood. The road to Mt Airy led through the most beautiful city park I had ever been in. Called Fairmount Park and covering almost 9,000 rolling acres, it is the largest municipal park in America and it is full of trees and fragrant shrubs and bosky glades of infinite charm. It stretches for miles along the banks of the Schuylkill River. We drove through a dreamy twilight. Boats sculled along the water. It was perfection.

Mt Airy was out in the Germantown section of the city. It had a nice settled feeling to it, as if people had lived there for generations – which is in fact the case in Philadelphia, Lucia told me. The city was still full of the sort of neighbourhoods where everybody knew everybody else. Many people scarcely ever ven-tured more than a few hundred yards from their homes. It was not uncommon to get lost and find that hardly anybody could reliably direct you to a neighbourhood three miles away. Philadelphia also had its own vocabulary – downtown was called centre city, sidewalks were called pavements, as in Britain – and peculiarities of pronunciation.

In the evening I sat in Hal and Lucia's house, eating their food, drinking their wine, admiring their children and their house and furniture and possessions, their easy wealth and comfort, and felt a sap for ever having left America. Life was so abundant here, so easy, so convenient. Suddenly I wanted a refrigerator that made its own ice-cubes and a waterproof radio for the shower. I wanted an electric orange juicer and a room ioniser and a wristwatch that would keep me in touch with my biorhythms. I wanted it all. Once in the evening I went upstairs to go to the bathroom and walked past one of the children's bedrooms. The door was open and a bedside light was on. There were toys everywhere – on the floor, on shelves, tumbling out of a wooden trunk. It looked like Santa's workshop. But there was nothing extraordinary about this, it was just a typical middle-class American bedroom.

And you should see American closets. They are always full of yesterday's enthusiasms: golf-clubs, scuba-diving equipment, tennis-rackets, exercise machines, tape recorders, dark-room equipment, objects that once excited their owner and then were replaced by other objects even more shiny and exciting. That is the great, seductive thing about America – the people always get what they want, right now, whether it is good for them or not. There is something deeply worrying, and awesomely irresponsible, about this endless self-gratification, this constant appeal to the baser instincts.

Do you want zillions off your state taxes even at the risk of crippling education?

'Oh, yes!' the people cry.

Do you want TV that would make an imbecile weep?

'Yes, please!'

Shall we indulge ourselves with the greatest orgy of consumer spending that the world has ever known?

'Sounds neat! Let's go for it!'

The whole of the global economy is based on supplying the cravings of two per cent of the world's population. If Americans suddenly stopped indulging themselves, or ran out of closet space, the world would fall apart. If you ask me, that's crazy.

I should point out that I am not talking about Hal and Lucia in all this. They are good people and lead modest and responsible lives. Their closets aren't full of scuba-diving equipment and seldom-used tennis-rackets. They are full of mundane items like buckets and galoshes, ear muffs and scouring powders. I know this for a fact because late in the night when everyone was asleep I crept out of bed and had a good look.

In the morning, I dropped Hal at his office downtown – correction, centre city – and the drive through Fairmount Park was as enchanting in the morning sunshine as it had been at dusk. All cities should have parks like this, I thought.

Further reading

Bill Bryson is well known for his humorous accounts of living and travelling in different parts of the world, especially the USA and Europe. Try his book *Notes from a Small Island* (Doubleday, 1995) to read what he says about the UK, and his impressions of cities here.

London

by William Blake

William Blake's short poem about London appeared in a collection of poetry published in 1794, *Songs of Innocence and Experience*. Blake cared passionately about the lives of the poor and downtrodden, and this can be seen in this short and simple work.

I wander thro' each charter'd[1] street,
Near where the charter'd Thames does flow,
And mark in every face I meet
Marks of weakness, marks of woe.

In every cry of every Man,
In every Infant's cry of fear,
In every voice, in every ban,[2]
The mind-forg'd manacles[3] I hear.

---

[1]**charter'd** there are at least two opposing meanings suggested here: 'chartered' can mean 'freed' or, conversely, 'limited and restricted' (in the sense of controlled, under a charter)
[2]**ban** prohibitions, or things you cannot do
[3]**manacles** handcuffs

How the Chimney-sweeper's cry
Every black'ning Church appalls;
And the hapless[4] soldier's sigh
Runs in blood down Palace walls.

But most thro' midnight streets I hear
How the youthful Harlot's curse
Blasts the new born Infant's tear,
And blights[5] with plagues the Marriage hearse.

Further reading

Read other poems by William Blake such as *Tyger, Tyger* or *A Poison Tree*, both taken from his collection *Songs of Innocence and Experience*. Both give a sense of his writing style, and his concerns and worries. *Blake* by Peter Ackroyd (Vintage, 1998) gives an insight into Blake's life and his struggles to get his voice heard.

---

[4]**hapless** unlucky
[5]**blights** harms

Composed upon Westminster Bridge
by William Wordsworth

Writing shortly after Blake, Wordsworth's sonnet from 1802, also about London, provides a very different image of the capital city as the poet gazes at the river below and the surrounding life.

Earth has not anything to show more fair:
Dull would he be of soul who could pass by
A sight so touching in its majesty:
This City now doth like a garment wear
The beauty of the morning; silent, bare,
Ships, towers, domes, theatres, and temples lie
Open unto the fields, and to the sky;
All bright and glittering in the smokeless air.
Never did sun more beautifully steep[1]
In his first splendour, valley, rock, or hill;
Ne'er saw I, never felt, a calm so deep!
The river glideth at his own sweet will:
Dear God! the very houses seem asleep;
And all that mighty heart is lying still!

Further reading

William Wordsworth is perhaps better known for his poetry related to the natural environment, especially the Lake District, where he lived for much of his life. *The Prelude* – a long, narrative poem – provides us with an account of his childhood and the influence of landscape on his thinking.

---

[1]**steep**   soak, bathe

Activities

Tokyo

Before you read

1   Have you ever woken up not knowing where you are, or in a place that is so dark you can't tell whether it's night or day? Talk about any experiences such as these in a small group before you begin reading.

What's it about?

2   Talk in pairs about whether you think Adam has been to Tokyo before. What evidence is there that he has or hasn't?

3   How does the author convey Adam's concerns about his situation? Think about his use of punctuation, for example.

4   What – or where – is Adam looking for? Why is he looking for this place?

5   After he has woken up, trace Adam's journey by writing down what he does as a series of bullet points: start . . .
   - Wakes up in sleeping 'pod'
   - Goes down to street

6   What problems does Adam have getting to his destination? Is everything difficult or are some things easier than he imagined?

Thinking about the text

7   We get a very strong sense of Adam's view of Tokyo from this extract. Pick out four or five key phrases or descriptions of the city as he sees it, and then add a short sentence summing up what overall picture we are given (e.g. 'Tokyo is described as a tranquil and welcoming place . . .').

8   Imagine you are a Japanese police officer investigating Charlie's disappearance. Looking at what you have found out about the situation, what do you think might have happened to her? Is her brother Adam right to be concerned, or is he just another foreigner who doesn't understand what Tokyo is like? Write a short report for your police chief suggesting what might have happened.

India: A Million Mutinies Now

Before you read

1   What do you understand by the word 'slum'? Have you seen reports from slums in different parts of the world? Discuss in pairs what these slums are usually like and what it must be like living in them.

What's it about?

2   In small groups, discuss the impression given of the slum of Dharavi from the time the writer leaves Papu's flat and returns to the 'Bombay of paved roads and buses . . .'. Are there particular words or phrases that stand out?

3   How close is the slum to where Papu lives? Find the specific sentence that tells you this information and note it down.

Thinking about the text

4   How keen is Papu to show the author the great slum? Think about what he says about the slum to start with before they leave the flat.

5   What can we learn about Papu's feelings about the slum later when they are travelling in the taxi?

6   Papu says that people say that those living in the slum are 'fundamentalists' (extremists – possibly terrorists), but then says, '. . . but don't you think you could make these people fight for anything you tell them to fight for?'. Discuss with a friend what you think he means by this.

7   Choosing some of the key images and descriptions of the slum, create a poem of 10 lines called 'Images of Dharavi'. If you can, make use of some of the repeated words and phrases from the text, such as 'black', and don't waste words unnecessarily: you could start . . .

Back-to-back, side-to-side,
Shacks and shelters, ragged lanes . . .

Pompeii

Before you read

1   Find out about the events in AD 79 when Pompeii and its sister city
Herculaneum were destroyed. Why is Pompeii one of the most visited tourist sites in the world nowadays? Is Mount Vesuvius (which
destroyed the city) still active and dangerous today?

What's it about?

2   In the novel, it is Attilius's job to keep the aqueducts and water
supplies flowing. Unfortunately he has discovered poisoned water
in another city in the Bay of Naples. Discuss in pairs how we can
tell from the first half of the text that he is worried about water in
Pompeii. What is his reaction when he comes to the fountain?

3   The extract includes a number of architectural terms describing
Roman buildings or places: 'basilica' and 'forum', for example.
Can you work out the meaning of either of these from the text? If
not, look them up and jot down their definitions.

4   Create a two-column table and at the top write the names 'Attilius'
and 'Corax'. Then, underneath each, jot down any information you
can find out about them from the text, and what this suggests
about them. For example:
Corax: Makes a private joke which he won't explain to Attilius.
Suggests: He laughs at people behind their backs, not to be trusted?

Thinking about the text

5   Turn the conversation between Attilius and Baculus, the horse-
dealer, into a short script. You will need to make sure you:
- set the scene with simple information (e.g. Scene 1: a market in
Pompeii. Enter . . .) and keep it in the *present tense*
- include the names on the left-hand side of the page
- add actions / movements / ways of speaking where needed.

6   Look again at the opening to the extract. Draw or sketch how
Pompeii appears to Attilius as his ship approaches Pompeii. Start
by jotting down any descriptions that will help you do your drawing (e.g. 'a fortress city . . .' ' . . . on higher ground . . .' ' . . . her
port beneath her . . .').

The Lost Continent

Before you read

1 Have you ever got lost and ended up in an unfamiliar place? How did it happen – and how did you feel? Did you meet anyone while you were lost? In groups, discuss your experiences.

What's it about?

2 How did Bill Bryson end up in the poorer neighbourhood in Philadelphia?

3 The text contains quite a lot of factual information. Working in small groups, go through the text and pick out any factual details about Philadelphia (numbers, dates, names of places etc. – but be careful: not details about other US cities).

4 Now, look through the text (up to ' . . . I don't know how they do it') and find descriptions of that part of Philadelphia Bryson ends up in at first, that tell us what he thinks of it. Then re-read the rest of the text – does he feel the same way about the rest of Philadelphia that he sees? Note down an example of a more positive description.

5 Bill Bryson is an American and some of the words he uses to describe things are different from the words we use in the UK. For example, 'trash' means 'rubbish', of course. He also uses 'stoop' and 'freeway'. Skim or scan the text to find these words, and see if you can work out their meanings (if you don't know them already). Can you find any others?

Thinking about the text

6 This text is not just about Philadelphia. Can you find other cities mentioned in the extract? Why does Bryson mention them?

7 Write a short imaginative story in which you get lost in an unfamiliar part of a town or city. Describe what you see (it needn't be poor or dangerous) and how you manage to leave. Describe the people and buildings as vividly as possible.

London

Before you read

1 What do you imagine life was like in London at the end of the 18th century, if you were poor? Discuss in groups the hardships you would face. What sort of jobs would have been available for the very poor?

What's it about?

2 Some of the words in the poem are explained in the glossary, but others aren't. Use a dictionary, thesaurus or Internet search engine to check your understanding of any unusual vocabulary.

3 Blake refers to several types of people in the poem. Who are they, and what seems to be his view of them? (Does he feel sympathy? anger?)

Thinking about the text

4 The poem has a regular rhyme scheme – what is the pattern? Why do you think Blake chose such a regular rhyme for such a serious subject? (Think about the title of the collection from which the poem comes.)

5 Re-read the poem and pick out the phrases or words that you think are most powerful. What do you think they tell us about Blake's attitude to London and the people who live there?

6 Research the life of a chimney-sweep in 18th-century London, and then write a diary of a day in his/her life. Remember to use the appropriate tense . . . **Today has been one of the most difficult in my young life** . . . and, if possible, imitate the style of a writer from the time:
   We were employed in a most frightful district, the like of which I have no desire to see again, for the soot and dirt were everywhere . . .

Composed upon Westminster Bridge

Before you read

1   Have you ever stood on a bridge and watched the waters flow past? Where was it – and at what time of day? How did it make you feel?

What's it about?

2   On your own, go through the poem and work out the rhyme scheme for it. For example, it begins with the first and fourth and second and third lines ending in rhymes. Does this pattern continue? When does it change?

3   From looking at the poem, do you think Wordsworth creates the impression he is gazing at the city and river *now* as he writes, or is he remembering the river much later, *looking back*?

4   There are a lot of positive descriptions in the poem. In pairs, make a list of them, and what they refer to (for example 'river'/'sweet').

5   Wordsworth uses a number of comparisons too. One is about the city and the morning – can you find it and explain what he is saying? Another refers to the houses. What impression is given by that comparison?

Thinking about the text

6   Wordsworth is writing about his view from the bridge in the early morning. Do you think he would have had a different feeling about the city at night-time?

7   Wordsworth refers to 'that mighty heart' in the last line of the poem. Whose heart is he referring to?

8   Think of any bridge (real or imagined) – it could be a large, concrete one over a motorway; a small, wooden one over a country stream; a pedestrian one over a river in a city – and write a description as if you were standing on it. Decide whether your feelings are positive about what you see (like Wordsworth) or negative.

Compare and contrast

1   Adam, in *Tokyo*, and Attilius, in *Pompeii*, are both newcomers to the two cities. Discuss in groups how they respond to the two places:
    ● Who seems more at home?
    ● What are their reasons for going to these cities?
    ● Are there any other differences or similarities between them? (Think about who they meet, and how they get what they want . . .).

When your group has finished discussing the two extracts, write up your findings on your own, supporting what you say with quotations or information from the text.

2   *India: A Million Mutinies Now* and *The Lost Continent* both present us with accounts of poor areas in cities. Write a short study of the ways V. S. Naipaul and Bill Bryson describe these areas.
    ● In what ways are the places similar?
    ● How are they different?
    ● Do the two authors respond in the same ways to them?

3   Compare and contrast the two poems *London* and *Composed upon Westminster Bridge*.
    ● What particular features of language do the poets use to convey their views of the city?
    ● Do they describe the same – or different – things about London?
    ● Which view do you find more convincing – and why?
Write up your conclusions as a short study.

4   Two of the extracts in this selection are from novels. In groups, look at the remaining three cities (Mumbai, Philadelphia and London) and situations.
    ● Discuss which would make the best setting for the start of a novel: the Dharavi slum in Mumbai, the Philadelphia suburbs, or London in the late 18th / early 19th century.
    ● Discuss who your central character could be and what he or she might be doing in this place.

2 This landscape, these people

This section focuses on people who are experiencing new places and people that are very different from where they have come from. In some cases, like *Spilled Water*, we meet people encountering built-up commercial areas for the first time. In others, such as *Entering the City* and *A Journey Back to My Hostage Hell*, people return to cities they once knew.

Activities

1 Think about novels, poems and stories you have read in which characters have moved from one very different environment to another. Make brief notes on their reactions to the new place, and the contrasts between it and the situation they have left – or are about to go back to.

2 Have you experienced moving from one place to another? This could be from school to school, or from country to town (or vice versa) – or even from one country to another one. How significant was the change for you – did you welcome it, or fear it – or perhaps both? How long did it take you to adjust to your new situation or place? Discuss these issues in your group.

3 Some of the extracts in this section deal with people returning to somewhere they grew up as a child. Do you think you will stay in the place where you currently live? What would you miss and not miss if you left? How do you think you would feel returning in ten years' time, for example? Make brief notes about these issues.

Spilled Water

by Sally Grindley

This extract is set in China and is about a girl, Lu Si-yan, who has run away from a family to whom she was sold by her uncle to be a servant. She has ended up working in a factory, trying to earn enough money to return to her home village. Here, she has gone with the other girls on their day off to the local town.

Once we had passed the industrial outskirts of the town and numerous grimy side streets crammed with cheerless single-storey shacks, we turned a corner and the road widened into a tawdry,[1] rackety shopping area. Multiple coloured neon lights flashed above the doorways and in the windows of the shops and eateries, even though it was still daylight. Music blared in a riot of competing tunes from shops selling jeans, cheap silk, ice creams, mobile phones and televisions. Hairdressers had chairs set out on the pavement regardless of the cold; there were mahjong[2] parlours, photo parlours and karaoke bars.

I was startled by the brashness[3] of it all. The market town I had visited with my father had been colourful and bustling, the town I had visited with Mrs Chen had been sparkling and elegant. Here was something different again. The centre of this town throbbed with exuberance, in stark contrast to the grim reality of life in its factories and streets. Certainly, the workers from the factories, as soon as they reached the shopping area, became like dogs let off the leash.

'Ice cream, ice cream, give me that lovely ice cream,' chanted Dong Ying.

We piled into a shop selling ice creams in eight tempting flavours.

---

[1] **tawdry**   showy, tasteless
[2] **mahjong**   a Chinese table game played with small painted tiles
[3] **brashness**   boldness

'I don't know which one to choose,' I said, desperate to avoid the disappointment of picking the least tasty.

'Choose more than one, then,' a boy in front turned to say. 'Who's counting?'

The thought of such extravagance made me blush, as did the mere fact of being spoken to by him, but then I saw that everyone ahead of me was coming away with three or four scoops.

'Spoil yourself,' said Dong Ying. 'You won't get many chances.'

'Not once the peak season begins,' grimaced Song Shuru.

I clutched the money that had been left in my locker. Whoever had given it to me had intended me to spend it on myself. I would start saving as soon as I received my own wages at the end of the week.

'Three scoops, please,' I said when I reached the front of the queue. 'Peach, vanilla and ginger.'

We walked slowly along the road, gazing at the clothes in the shops, licking at our ice creams, which would have tasted delicious after the food at the factory even if I hadn't made the best choice. Dong Ying darted into one shop to try on a jumper. While we waited, we browsed through the racks of blouses, skirts and trousers. Li Mei pounced on a long-sleeved yellow blouse and held it up against me.

'This was made for you, Lu Si-yan. When you earn your first wages you must come into town and buy it.'

The other girls nodded enthusiastic agreement.

I looked at myself in a mirror, astonished to see how I had changed again. I was very thin, but my eyes sparkled with excitement and my cheeks were pink from the cold wind. The yellow blouse suited me. How I wished I could buy it, but I had only just committed myself to saving as soon as I received my first wage packet. Then again, I thought, I couldn't expect to borrow my friends' clothes all the time. Having a valid reason[4] to buy

---

[4]**valid reason**   good reason for doing something, justifiable

the blouse made me glow with pleasure momentarily, for I had never bought any clothes for myself before. And I told myself that the blouse was so cheap that it would eat up only a tiny amount of my wages.

We strolled in and out of shops all along the road. None of us had much money to spend, but we were happy to dream and to watch other people. The long hours and the monotony of their jobs made many of the factory workers reckless and extravagant when they found themselves suddenly free to do as they liked. The shopkeepers, reliant upon these once-weekly shopping sprees to feed their families, cajoled[5] and encouraged us through their doors in the hopes of making a sale. The result was a carnival atmosphere, exuberant and infectious.

Li Mei linked her arm through mine.

'Come on, young lady,' she grinned. 'Let's go and sing.'

She pulled me towards a karaoke bar, urged on by Dong Ying and Song Shuru.

'I can't sing,' I protested, laughing.

'Of course you can,' coaxed Li Mei. 'We'll sing together.'

'But you're too good.'

'Singing is freedom and happiness. Today you are free and happy. Sing, Lu Si-yan.'

The darkened bar was crowded with people, even though it was the middle of the afternoon. Coloured spotlights lit a small platform where a young man was crooning and gyrating to an over-loud backing track. I put my fingers in my ears. I had never seen or heard anything like it.

'Nothing could be worse than that,' shouted Shen Enqing. 'For goodness sake put him out of his misery, Li Mei.'

'As soon as he's finished then, Lu Si-yan,' yelled Li Mei.

She went over to the man in charge of the karaoke machine and whispered something in his ear. He nodded and, after a few seconds, slowly faded out the previous music. The young man leapt from the platform to mocking applause, while Li Mei

---

[5]**cajoled**   persuaded

pulled me up in his place. The strains of a new tune gradually became audible and I realised that it was one of my father's favourites.

'I've heard you humming it,' grinned Li Mei. 'Let's show them how it's done.'

I couldn't believe I was standing up there in front of dozens of people I didn't know. I wanted to run away and hide. My heart thumped wildly, I felt sick. But when Li Mei began to sing, I found myself joining in, at first shyly, then, as the music took over, with more and more assurance. Dong Ying, Song Shuru and Shen Enqing danced exotically[6] in front of us. People tapped their feet, rapped on the bar, clapped their hands. Attracted by the commotion, passers-by crammed into the entrance of the bar and joined in as well. The music reached a crescendo, Li Mei turned to me, and we shouted out the last notes smiling broadly at each other. It was exhilarating, and I loved it.

When the music came to an end, the crowd clapped wildly, shouting for more. Li Mei called over to the karaoke man. The opening strains of another of my father's favourites filtered through to me above the clamour. Li Mei laughed at the expression of amazement on my face, then we began again. I poured myself into the song, recalling precious fragments from my past, cherishing my friends who were my present.

Further reading

If you enjoyed this extract, you might like to read *Chinese Cinderella: The true story of an unwanted daughter* by Adeline Yen Mah (Puffin Books, 1998), an autobiographical account of a Chinese girl's upbringing some years earlier. Her hardships are somewhat different, but are also about being alone and trying to survive.

---

[6]**exotically**   in a way that seemed foreign, not in a traditional way

No Turning Back

by Beverley Naidoo

This extract, taken from Beverley Naidoo's novel about South Africa, *No Turning Back*, is about a boy named Sipho who has run away from home in a township to look for work in Johannesburg and has ended up with a group of homeless street children begging. In this extract, Sipho follows the others as they try to raise money and find a safe place to sleep for the night.

The rest of the afternoon was spent criss-crossing Hillbrow with Jabu, Matthew and Thabo, going nowhere in particular. The others let Sipho wander along the pavement market stalls without rushing him. He was curious about everything. Leather bags, purses, cassette tapes, shampoo, combs, cigarettes, matches, coloured groundnuts,[1] wooden carvings, necklaces and bracelets made of beads . . . all of these things were spread out neatly on tables or blankets. Worried about being chased away, Sipho was careful not to go too close. Instead he watched customers pick up items and examine them before buying or bargaining with the trader. Sometimes the four of them shared a joke at what they saw.

They had stopped to follow some bargaining between a trader and customer when Sipho's eyes were drawn to a nearby table full of carvings. He had to stop himself from putting out his hand. Among the masks and heads carved in wood and stone stood a line of small wooden animals. Because they were small, he needed to peer closely at them. An almost black rhino with two horns, one big and one small, seemed to be running. One back leg was raised off the table. As Sipho crouched down to see it better, the creature seemed to stare at him from the black dot in the middle of its tiny white eye. He thought it appeared a little worried. Behind it was a fat elephant with its

---

[1]**groundnuts**   peanuts

trunk in the air that made him want to laugh. The colour of the wood had given it brown stripes! If only he could pick them up and feel them. Like he did with the clay animals he used to make from red earth on the farm. Would the rhino stare at him from his other eye too? And would that eye be scared or fierce?

'You want to buy one? I'll give you a good deal. Only ten rand[2].'

The trader's voice startled him and he looked up into the face of a man whose skin appeared as deeply polished as the wood of the rhino.

'I like the rhino *baba*,[3] but I don't have money.'

'Maybe you will earn it and come back one day, young man.'

'*Yebo*,[4] *baba*. I will try.'

Casting a last glance at the animals, Sipho forced himself to leave and go back to the others.

Further down the road at a shoe-repair shop, Matthew handed Thabo the empty plastic bottle from his pocket, counted out five rand and went inside. When he came back he was carrying a small tin. Moving into a narrow alley nearby, Matthew carefully poured the white liquid from the tin into the bottle. Sipho knew it was glue.[5] A boy at school had been expelled for selling it.

When Matthew and Thabo said they wanted to sit down for a while, Sipho asked Jabu if he could 'park cars'[6] with him. The pangs of hunger were now gripping him more tightly. They were lucky and after about half an hour had earned enough money to buy chips from a fast-food shop. Still eating, they joined a crowd surrounding two men playing *umrabaraba*[7] with

---

[2]**rand**   South African currency
[3]*baba*   a respectful term when addressing an older person
[4]*yebo*   yes
[5]**glue**   some of the street children sniffed glue
[6]**park cars**   the boys made money by offering to park and look after people's cars
[7]*umrabaraba*   a traditional African game played with counters or small stones

counters on the pavement. Matthew and Thabo were there too. Matthew was giggling but Thabo was silent. It was a noisy game, full of drama. One player was accused of cheating because an onlooker had given him advice. Soon all the adults seemed to have taken sides. Worried that a fight might break out, the four boys slipped away from the centre. A minute later, however, the argument was over and the boys wandered off.

Later in the afternoon they made their way down a hill to a busy junction, along which people travelled home from the city. At first Sipho stayed on the side, watching the other three as they walked in between the rows of cars at the traffic lights, asking for money. The queues were long and they had to dart out of the way just before the lights turned green.

Plucking up courage, he went further down the road and when the cars began to slow down he slipped in between them. A lot of the drivers kept looking ahead as if he wasn't even there. Their windows were tightly shut but every now and again someone would roll down the window and drop a coin into his hands. In some cars there were children who stared at him from the back seats. However, when two children in school uniform – a girl and a boy – stuck out their tongues, Sipho pulled a face back. At first they looked surprised and he saw them say something to their mother. As she turned to glare at Sipho, the car behind her hooted. Her face twitched suddenly. The lights had turned green and Sipho had to dash to the side!

The sun was going down, leaving deep red and purple stripes in the sky above the buildings on top of the hill. All the buildings had turned a shadowy grey. A light wind was beginning to blow and Sipho felt the chill go right through him. Once again, he wished he had remembered to bring a second jumper with him before leaving home. Taking out the woolly cap he had stuffed into his pocket earlier in the day, he pulled it down over his head and ears. Jogging up and down also helped, especially when the lights were green and he had to stand aside as the cars swept by.

He was beginning to wonder when the others would want to move on, when he heard a high-pitched whistle from behind him. He swung around to see Jabu, Thabo and Matthew already on the road back up to Hillbrow. Jabu was signalling to him. When Sipho joined them, they were exchanging news on their earnings. No one had earned more than a couple of rand. Thabo had been given a packet of crisps and he shared them as they walked. Sipho told them about how he had pulled a face back at the rude schoolchildren.

'The school kids in the bus sometimes throw rubbish down on us!' Matthew told Sipho.

'Just let them show off their turkey-tails[8] on the street. Then you'll hear them shriek when we pull out their feathers!' boasted Thabo.

---

[8]**turkey-tails**   an unflattering description, rather like calling someone 'chicken', meaning a coward

They walked quickly uphill. Jabu said that people in the bakery would be clearing up and they could buy any left-over bread cheaply. They arrived just in time. The front of the shop was closed but the back door was still open and they went inside. The manager seemed annoyed when he saw them.

'Do you think I want to stay here all night?' he complained.

But he took the money they offered and came back with two packets of rolls and a small loaf of bread.

'This is all that's left. You'll have to share. Now move on!'

Outside the bakery, Sipho listened as the others discussed whether to go directly back to the *pozzie* – their sleeping-place. If Lucas was there, he might have made a fire and at least they would be warmer there. Sipho was glad when they agreed to go. Already, he was very tired. He hoped that when it was time to sleep he would be too tired to feel the cold.

Starting to walk downhill again, Jabu explained to Sipho that their gang had recently stopped sleeping in Hillbrow.

'The police chase us too much here,' he told Sipho.

'And if the shopkeeper finds you in the morning by his door, sometimes he'll beat you ... shuup, shuup, shuup!' added Matthew, whipping his arm up and down.

Two weeks ago, however, Lucas had found a small unused plot of ground near the railway line at Doornfontein where they could sleep. The only problem was that hoboes[9] sometimes came to the plot to drink. The drinking often led to fighting and the boys were worried the police would then come and take them all away. But at least Lucas had claimed one side of the plot for the *malunde*[10] and the hoboes stayed on the other side. Sipho thought of the man who had sworn at him that morning and hoped he wouldn't be there.

The streets were now brightly lit up. Even high above, the darkness of the night was broken by lights in the buildings towering upwards. If he had been going back home through the

---

[9]**hoboes**   tramps; adults living on the street
[10]*malunde*   street children

shacks in the township[11] at this time, everything would be completely dark. When there was no moon, you had to fumble your way as best you could between the shacks. Here there were even shops still open with lots of people walking around. Music drifted out from some of the cafés and bars. In the roads cars were pulling up or moving out, just as busy as during the day. However, the further they walked down the hill, the quieter and darker it became.

At the bottom, they turned left. They were beginning to leave the very tall buildings behind. The wind rustled the leaves in the trees above them, and shadows seemed to dance around them as they moved from one pool of lamplight to the next. Jabu told Sipho that behind them was a park which was very dangerous, even in daytime. *Tsotsis*[12] hung around there and sometimes they would take one of the *malunde* if they wanted him for a robbery or some other bad thing.

'OK, we also steal sometimes if we're hungry or need something,' said Jabu, 'but those *tsotsis*, they actually *like* killing!'

'*Ja*, and they like telling everyone how they cut up this one and stabbed that one,' added Matthew.

As they turned into a narrower road without any traffic, Sipho could hear the sound of their footsteps. The others were now talking about a man called Peter who liked to finger his knife while forcing *malunde* to buy glue from him. A couple of times Sipho turned around to make sure no one was following them.

Further reading

Beverley Naidoo has written several novels about life for children in South Africa. You might like to read *Journey to Jo'burg* (Longman, 1985) and its sequel *Chain of Fire* (Puffin Books, 2004) about two children's journey to find their mother who is working 200 miles away in the city.

---

[11]**township**   that part of a South African city where poorer black people live
[12]**tsotsis**   street gangsters

The Ruined Maid

by Thomas Hardy

Hardy's poem, probably written in 1866, is a dialogue between two country girls, one of whom has left the countryside to live in the town/city and has changed quite a bit as a result!

'O 'Melia, my dear, this does everything crown!
Who could have supposed I should meet you in Town?
And whence such fair garments, such prosperi-ty?' –
'O didn't you know I'd been ruined?' said she.

'You left us in tatters, without shoes or socks,
Tired of digging potatoes, and spudding[1] up docks;
And now you've gay bracelets and bright feathers three!' –
'Yes: that's how we dress when we're ruined,' said she.

---

[1]**spudding** digging

– 'At home in the barton[2] you said "thee" and "thou,"
And "thik oon," and "theäs oon," and "t'other"; but now
Your talking quite fits 'ee for high compa-ny!' –
'Some polish is gained with one's ruin,' said she.

– 'Your hands were like paws then, your face blue and bleak
But now I'm bewitched by your delicate cheek,
And your little gloves fit as on any la-dy!' –
'We never do work when we're ruined,' said she.

– 'You used to call home-life a hag-ridden[3] dream,
And you'd sigh, and you'd sock; but at present you seem
To know not of megrims[4] or melancho-ly!' –
'True. One's pretty lively when ruined,' said she.

– 'I wish I had feathers, a fine sweeping gown,
And a delicate face, and could strut about Town!' –
'My dear – a raw country girl, such as you be,
Cannot quite expect that. You ain't ruined,' said she.

Further reading

Thomas Hardy's novels also deal with 'ruined' women – most notably
Tess of the D'Urbervilles in which a young, pretty milkmaid is seduced by
a local landowner and has to face the consequences.

The style of the poem – a form of dialogue – is one adopted by
other poets, too. A famous example which uses this approach is the
anonymous *Edward, Edward* written in Scottish dialect in which a
mother questions a son about the blood on his hands until he reveals
the terrible deeds he has committed!

---

[2]**barton**   farmyard
[3]**hag-ridden**   troubled by nightmares
[4]**megrims**   migraines

Estates

by Lynsey Hanley

In this extract the author revisits the estate where she grew up, close to the centre of Birmingham, England's second largest city. She explains its layout and appearance and how it affects the people who live there, at the same time recalling her own childhood and how she viewed it then.

The road my parents live on is on the extreme south-eastern border of the estate: a long, boomerang-shaped crescent from which car-free stalks of terrace housing spring out. Everywhere you look there are houses. There are no high-rise flats in this neck of the Wood, only criss-crossing macadamed walks with boxy brown rows set on either side. In the early days, people would regularly get lost looking for their own houses, such was the uniformity of the housing and the complexity of its design.

When I picture my parents' home – its position, its plot, its proximity to this and that – I think of all the other houses it so closely resembles in the immediate area. I keep thinking of the same word: square. Square and solid shapes, 18,000 times over, laid out in lines and curves that lead into each other like a never-ending maze. Their home – the house I lived in from the age of nine until I moved to London aged eighteen – is square and solid, and without embellishment. It's made from sandy brick, a three-bed semi, with a front lawn about the size of an adult's armspan and a drive that has never housed a car. Unlike most of its neighbours, it doesn't have an awning or a porch, and its windows were free of net curtains until the time it was burgled twice in a month. Its pitched roof makes it seem proud, if not handsome (flat-roofed houses look to me like headless bodies). Inside it has been improved and improved again, with a knocked-through wall to make the living room long and lean, a buff-coloured Ikea kitchen, and a wheat-coloured carpet that shows up every speck of dust.

A peacock chair[1] holds court in one corner next to the telly, on which a collection of battery-stomached[2] cuddly toys talk and gurgle on demand. I squash them by sitting on them and look sideways out of the front window, just as I used to do when I was waiting for my mum to get back from work on long afternoons in the holidays. Shrek[3] mumbles something sage about onions into the small of my back. I see a narrowish road quietened by speed bumps and the deep red row of two-bed terrace houses, as flat-fronted as pancakes on a washing line, that sit on the other side of it. This is the quiet, nice end of the estate; very nearly *rus in urbe*,[4] backed not by further rows of square semis and two-bed terraces but by the vast gardens of those

---

[1]**peacock chair**   a particular design of high-backed chair made in the Far East, popular in the 1970s
[2]**battery-stomached**   the toys had internal batteries to make them work
[3]**Shrek**   one of the cuddly toys; a film character
[4]***rus in urbe***   countryside in the city

whom I only know as the posh people, whose desire not to be reminded that they are bordered by a council estate has led them to grow forty-foot-high walls of coniferous trees that starve my parents' own plants of light.

The only thing that reminds you of where you are, and how you came to be there, is the wind. When it blows in the wrong direction, towards the house, the trickle of the goldfish pond and the twirrup of the birds gives way to the modern-day roar of the M6, M42 and M45 motorways, which converge less than a mile away. Then there is the grating pulse of inter-city trains a further mile from that, and the thrust of engines from the adjacent airport. They say it's handy for transport links: handy if you've got a car or if you fancy going to Toronto or Cancun,[5] but less so if haven't and you want to visit friends down the road on a Sunday. Neither I, my parents, nor my grandparents have ever owned a car; a doubly strange feat in an area whose main source of skilled employment is the motor industry. Fresh lines of newish Ford Focuses (for the men) and Ford Kas (for the women) seem to crop up on this road every day, making my parents seem ever odder for their complete reliance on public transport. 'I've got better things to spend me money on,' says my dad, meaning that if he were to run a car he would never be able to afford to go on holiday, and to him and my mum (and to me), holidays are sacrosanct.[6]

My nan, who has never strayed beyond England and Wales, lives fifty steps away from my mum and dad, on one of the pedestrianized culs-de-sac,[7] in an end-of-terrace house that is also square and without embellishment. Hers is built with a creamy, lighter tone of brick that matches the dozen in her row, most of which have now been bought from the council and enhanced with brown-paned double-glazed windows and

---

[5]**Toronto or Cancun**   cities far away (in Canada and Mexico)
[6]**sacrosanct**   very special, even holy or sacred
[7]**culs-de-sac**   roads with only one entrance; dead ends

clear-panelled doors with little stained-glass tulips at eye height. Behind, there is a fair patch of garden, about fifteen feet by fifteen, where once she grew strawberries and green beans. I thought my memory had betrayed me when I remembered being able to see out from her garden to the redundant lump of green space on to which a four-sided barrage of backyard gates opened: her eight-foot-high fence looks pretty old these days. But then my mum reminds me how none of the houses with gardens had their own fences for several years, until the tedium of fetching footballs from one end of the green expanse – now potholed with shrubbery in order to prevent children from playing there – to the other became too much, and tenants were allowed to erect dividing fences.

The strange thing about the Wood is that it's so large, and yet in the course of my life I feel like I've traversed[8] nearly every one of its roads and 'stalks' at least once. It's warren-like and labyrinthine,[9] and yet so hideously familiar that I want to see if I can take the most complicated walk I can without getting lost. It's still light; I've got nothing to lose but a digital camera which I keep under wraps, not for fear of mugging, but of looking even more of an outsider than I do already.

The estate splashes itself over four pages of the *A to Z*,[10] but I ignore the map and start with a journey I could make blindfolded, even though I haven't covered the route for eighteen years. I'm going to walk to my old primary school. The sky is bright blue and blustery, making the very sharp squareness of everything I see look beautiful and ordered. I smile at an elderly woman walking her rug-like dog and she smiles back; today, the Wood is good. Passing my nan's house, I absent-mindedly close her front gate and note a police sign, the colour of banana

---

[8]**traversed**   crossed
[9]**labyrinthine**   like a maze
[10]***A to Z***   a book of maps showing all the streets and important features of a large city

skins, stating that car crime in this area is higher than average. Quite what action or emotion this statement is designed to induce, apart from paranoia,[11] is beyond me, but I shuffle on in my metropolitan[12] corduroy jeans and sensible hat, past the broken-down fence and along the side of the now defunct play area. Once, when I was about four, a slightly smaller boy tried to trip me up with his foot while I was riding my first bike along this path, and was rewarded with a right earful from my mum. When I was a child, I used to walk down blind alleys in the gaps between terraces; as an adult, I flash my eyes up and down like danger-detectors. The bright lights flick on one by one in the square windows of the square houses. I have been walking for thirty seconds, and have passed thirty households.

Five minutes later – five turns along short interlocking paths, and a hundred-odd homes, half a dozen terrace houses and a Battenburg-cake[13] layer of one-bedroom flats on either side of the walkway, with a bollard at each end – I come to my first road. I look back at the domino contest I've just passed through and realize exactly what fascinates me about the estate I grew up on: it's all houses. That's what it is: houses everywhere, without a break. That's what it's there for. That's the only reason it's there.

Further reading

Lynsey Hanley's book *Estates* (Granta, 2007) from which this comes not only deals with the estate in the extract but others across the UK too, and what it is like living in them – with some good, some not-so-good experiences. Another book that deals with what it is like living in communities is Tobias Jones's *Utopian Dreams* (Faber and Faber, 2008) in which he lives in five different communities around the world, comparing their lifestyles and environments.

---

[11]**paranoia**   a mental condition that makes a person suspicious of everyone
[12]**metropolitan**   related to modern city living and culture
[13]**Battenburg cake**   a cake which, in cross-section, is made up of four alternating blocks of pink and yellow sponge

A Home from Home

by George Alagiah

In this extract, George Alagiah, a BBC newsreader and reporter whose family were themselves immigrants, describes the appeal of America to the millions of people who arrived at Ellis Island throughout the 19th and 20th centuries. He visits an area of Manhattan, once rumoured to be the 'most crowded place on earth'.

The statue's special resonance for immigrants comes from the lines of a poem written by one Emma Lazarus. The lines now immortalised at the base of the monument are like a nineteenth-century mission statement[1] for America. Its last lines are as emotive today as they were on the day a New York philanthropist discovered them amongst a number of other poems commissioned as part of the original fund-raising drive to erect the statue:

Give me your tired, your poor,
Your huddled masses yearning to breathe free,
The wretched refuse of your teeming shore,
Send these, the homeless, tempest-tossed, to me:
I lift my lamp beside the golden door.

The plaque with Emma Lazarus's poem was fixed to the statue's pedestal in 1903, three years before the Greig family were ferried towards Manhattan. From where they were, they would not have been able to read the words, but as they turned their gaze from Liberty towards the approaching shoreline, they would have been dumbstruck by the skyline that seemed to rise from the very waters of the Hudson.[2] It truly must have felt like a New World. The majesty of the buildings must have spoken

---

[1]**mission statement**   stated goals, usually of a business or other large organisation
[2]**Hudson**   the river that flows into the sea at New York

more eloquently than words of the city's unabashed dedication to wealth creation. They may have seen the Singer Building going up. When it was finished the following year, it would reach forty-seven storeys high! London's Canary Wharf, built nearly a century later in 1991, only has three more floors.

How do I know so much about the Greig family and their fellow passengers? Well, I may have made up the bit about poor old Telford being dragged away (though he was on the *Columbia*), but the rest of it is true. Names, dates, manifest[3] numbers – it's all available at the click of a mouse. Today Ellis Island is a spectacularly conceived museum, with an online database into which thousands of ships' manifests and other immigration papers have been transferred. This is not a museum full of preserved exhibits in glass boxes, but a living tribute to immigration. In his hugely accessible book on Ellis Island,[4] *Immigration's Shining Centre*, John Cunningham says that 'immigration is America's basic story, the source of the nation's strength and its uniqueness'. It's thought that 100 million Americans – that's roughly one in three of them – can trace their forebears back to this island. This is a place where Americans are encouraged to delve into their past.

Mary Greig's granddaughter is one of them. Her name is Susan Hess and she had just confirmed the Ellis Island connection when I met her. 'It's just so exciting,' she said, palpably moved by her discovery. 'We must have got about two hundred hits on the website.' Susan and her husband now live in Irvine, California, modern-day versions of the westward drift that started at Ellis Island in another age. The fact that they had travelled all the way from their home near the Pacific coastline – a continent away – to see Ellis Island tells you a great deal about

---

[3]**manifest**   a list of passengers and/or freight being carried by a ship on a particular journey

[4]**Ellis Island**   the island in New York harbour on which the Statue of Liberty stands; also the point of entry to America for immigrants from Europe in the 19th century and first half of the 20th century

Americans' attitude to immigration. It is something to be celebrated, not something to tolerate.

Outside, in the grounds of Ellis Island, is a 'wall of honour'. In return for a donation, people can have the names of their Ellis Island ancestors inscribed on shining steel panels that radiate out towards the Hudson River. From Leigh Ann Aaberg on panel 7 through Ramnath Lakshmiratam and Kee-Lim Li Chai to Wladislaw P. Zyzyk on panel 578, there are thousands of names. They came as individuals and families, but on this memorial they are brought together. They arrived as Austrians, Lithuanians, Indians, Chinese and Polish, but by the time they passed on the baton to the next generation, they were Americans. The message behind this wall of honour is clear: to have had a relation, however distant, come through this place is a privilege. Immigration is a privilege, it is a good thing.

About a third of the many millions who came through Ellis Island settled in New York itself. At the turn of the last century the little corner of Manhattan south of about Rivington Street and east of Bowery was reckoned to be the most crowded place on earth. Wave after wave of migrants headed into the district. Irish, Polish, Germans, Ukrainians and Russians, many of them Jews fleeing the European pogroms,[5] jostled for accommodation and jobs in what is now known as the Lower East Side. Most ended up in the garment business. Whole families would sit around the kitchen table sewing a batch of 'knee pants', otherwise known as knickerbockers. After a while the father of the household might move up the chain, becoming a 'sweater' who contracted out small orders to other, newer immigrants. The Far East sweatshops of today are just bigger and more efficient versions of the teeming tenements of nineteenth-century New York.

Number 97 Orchard Street is one such tenement building. Between 1863 and 1935, when the last tenants were evicted, some 7,000 immigrants from twenty countries had passed

---

[5]**pogroms**   organised massacres of a group of people (usually Jews)

through its door. Like those rock exhibits that show the different strata that make up a geological formation, 97 Orchard Street is a cutaway of America's immigrant past. It, too, is now a museum.

Among the earliest residents were Julius and Nathalie Gumpertz, who had settled into one of the apartments by 1870. Both were Prussian immigrants who had arrived in New York separately. Julius was a shoemaker. In their three-roomed flat (only one was designated as a bedroom; the other two were parlour and kitchen respectively) they brought up their four children – Rosa, Nannie, Olga and Isaac. On 7 October 1874, at seven o'clock in the morning, Julius set off for work as usual. He never returned and the family never found out what happened to him. Nathalie became the sole breadwinner. Like 35,000 other people in the city at the time she became a dressmaker. Her front room, the only one with natural light, was a workshop during the day, a sitting room when it needed to be one and a bedroom at night.

Among the last tenants at 97 Orchard Street were the Baldizzi family. Adolfo Baldizzi, a cabinet-maker from Palermo in Sicily, made his passage to the New World as a stowaway on a ship in 1923. A year later his wife Rosaria joined him. They lived at number 97 from 1928 to 1935. Adolfo and Rosaria had two children. One of them, Josephine, lived to see the opening of the museum in 1989. In the book published by the museum, *A Tenement Story*, she gives her reaction to how much the area had changed in the fifty years since the Baldizzis had moved on: 'When I came in contact with the immigrants coming here now I said, "Oh my God what country am I in. These are all foreign people. What are they all doing here." Then I realised that these poor immigrants now are doing the same things my parents did.'

Indeed the area has changed, subject to the constant metamorphosis[6] that is both the muddle and the marvel of

---

[6]**metamorphosis**   a radical transformation; specifically it is the process by which a caterpillar changes into a butterfly

migration. When I rented an apartment on Rivington with my wife, Frances, and our sons so I could do a bit of research for this book, the area seemed more Hispanic[7] than anything else. From our overheated flat we looked out on the Havana newsagent where, of all things, you could pick up a plate of sushi to go.[8] Across the street was PS 140 (in a triumph of order over imagination, all the public schools run by the education department are given a number). To be fair, the sign also said *Nathan Straus School*. The Straus family had emigrated from Rhenish Bavaria, today's Germany, in the early 1850s. Nathan, a shrewd businessman, would go on to open Macy's at Herald Square, which was dubbed the 'world's largest deparment store'. In 2005, the head teacher at the school was Esteban Barrientos. What will his pupils leave to posterity?

All immigrants help to shape the countries they land in, but in America their influence seems to have been felt more quickly and deeply (and in the case of the native Indians, more savagely) than in Britain. That most quintessential of American songs, the hand-on-heart 'God Bless America', was penned by a Russian immigrant whose family had arrived in the country in 1888. Born Israel Baline, legend has it that a printer's error gave him the name that will forever be associated with popular entertainment in America – Irving Berlin. If ever you want an outpouring of patriotism, this is it:

God bless America, land that I love.
Stand beside her and guide her
Through the night with a light from above.
From the mountains, to the prairies,
To the oceans white with foam
God bless America,
My home sweet home.

---

[7]**Hispanic**   referring to people from the Caribbean islands that were colonised by the Spanish, e.g. Cuba, Puerto Rico
[8]**sushi to go**   take-away fast food, Japanese style; sushi is raw fish

Written in cold black and white the words seem tacky[9] and the tune mundane.[10] Hear it sung, as I have standing in a large crowd outside St Patrick's Cathedral on Madison Avenue in New York, after the attacks on that city and Washington in 2001, and you understand the emotive hold this song has on Americans.

It was another turn-of-the-century immigrant who first came up with the phrase that for decades encapsulated America's apparent ability to absorb millions of immigrants with such differing traditions and turn them into the kind of people who would all sing 'God Bless America' and, what's more, mean every word of it! In 1908 a play by one Israel Zangwill, a Jewish immigrant from England, was first performed in Washington. Apart from the aficionados,[11] nobody remembers the plot but everybody knows the title. It was called *The Melting Pot*. I've often wondered what words Zangwill might have found to describe the immigrant experience in Britain, where he lived and worked before moving to America. Clearly he found some inspiration there that was lacking in Hackney, east London.

Whether the 'melting pot' is any longer a credible metaphor for America's race relations is a hotly debated subject. There, too, people are beginning to question the model, seeing it replaced by what some call the 'hyphenated' identity. There are fears that instead of the one America of apple-pie fame, the country is splitting into factions based on ethnicity. So you have African-Americans, Italian-Americans, Asian-Americans and the like. The counter argument is that in all these descriptions being American remains the baseline. In fact some of this was prefigured in another theatrical production, this time a Broadway musical of the late fifties. *West Side Story* came closest to illuminating the modern immigrant experience

---

[9]**tacky**   showing poor taste or style
[10]**mundane**   dull, ordinary
[11]**aficionados**   experts, devoted fans, usually of a sport

in America. It was huge on stage and an even bigger sensation when it was made into a film in 1961. It went on to win ten Oscars.

Based in the New York of the fifties, it was a contemporary rendition[12] of a much older love story, Shakespeare's *Romeo and Juliet*. In this version, though, the rivalry between the Montagus and Capulets is rendered into an Upper West Side feud between two gangs – one drawn from established European immigrants, the other from the more recent arrivals, the Puerto Ricans. One of its signature tunes is 'America' in which the entire Puerto Rican half of the cast is assembled on a rooftop. It is a biting and deeply ironic take on the American dream. If one character presents the best of America, another shoots back with its darker side. Listen to this:

ANITA: *Skyscrapers bloom in America*
ROSALIA: *Cadillacs[13] zoom in America*
GIRLS: *Industry boom in America*
BOYS: *Twelve in a room in America*
ANITA: *Life can be bright in America*
BOYS: *If you can fight in America*
GIRLS: *Life is all right in America*
BOYS: *If you're all white in America*

The song is remarkable for its honesty, particularly given Hollywood's predilection[14] for sanitising everything it touches – especially in the late fifties and sixties.

Now, whether you are of the *Melting Pot* school of thought or more partial to the *West Side Story* interpretation of the immigrant experience in America, you have to be impressed by the extent to which the subject has provided such a strong and enduring narrative to the country's popular culture.

---

[12]**rendition**   an interpretation, in song, dance or drama
[13]**Cadillacs**   large, flashy American cars especially popular in the mid-20th century
[14]**predilection**   preference

Further reading

Another former BBC news reporter, Rageh Omaar, has also written about the immigrant experience in his book *Only Half of Me: Being a Muslim in Britain* (Penguin, 2007), in which he describes his own childhood growing up in London.

This Landscape, These People
by Zulfikar Ghose

Zulfikar Ghose describes the experience of living in the UK and looks back at his childhood in India.

I

My eighth spring in England I walk among
   The silver birches of Putney Heath,
   Stepping over twigs and stones: being stranger,
   I see but do not touch: only the earth
   Permits an attachment. I do not wish
To be seen, and move, eyes at my sides, like a fish.

And do they notice me, I wonder, these
   Englishmen strolling with stiff country strides?
   I lean against a tree, my eyes are knots
   In its bark, my skin the wrinkles in its sides.
   I leap hedges, duck under chestnut boughs,
And through the black clay let my swift heels trail like ploughs.

A child at a museum, England for me
   Is an exhibit within a glass case.
   The country, like an antique chair, has a rope
   Across it. I may not sit, only pace
   Its frontiers. I slip through ponds, jump ditches,
Through galleries of ferns see England in pictures.

II

My seventeen years in India, I swam
   Along the silver beaches of Bombay,
   Pulled coconuts from the sky and tramped
   Red horizons with the swagger and sway
   Of Romantic youth; with the impudence
Of a native tongue, I cried for independence.

A troupe[1] came to town, marched through villages;
   Began with two tight-rope walkers, eyes gay
   And bamboos and rope on their bare shoulders;
   A snake-charmer joined them, beard long and grey,
   Baskets of cobras[2] on his turbaned head;
Through villages marched: children, beating on drums, led

Them from village to village, and jugglers
   Joined them and swallowers of swords, eaters
   Of fire brandishing flames through the thick air,
   Jesters with tongues obscene[3] as crows', creatures
   Of the earth: stray dogs, lean jackals, a cow;
Stamping, shouting, entertaining, making a row

---

[1]**troupe**   a group of performers
[2]**cobra**   a snake used by snake charmers in India for entertainment
[3]**tongues obscene**   saying naughty or rude things

From village to village they marched to town;
  Conjurors to bake bread out of earth, poets
  To recite epics[4] at night. The troupe, grown
  Into a nation, halted, squirmed: the sets
  For its act, though improvised, were re-cast
From the frames of an antique, slow-moving, dead past.

India halted: as suddenly as a dog,
  Barking, hangs out his tongue, stifles his cry.
  An epic turned into a monologue[5]
  Of death. The rope lay stiff across the country;
  All fires were eaten, swallowed all the swords;
The horizons paled, then thickened, blackened with crows.

Born to this continent, all was mine
  To pluck and taste: pomegranates to purple
  My tongue and chillies to burn my mouth. Stones
  Were there to kick. This landscape, these people –
  Bound by the rope and consumed by their own fire.
Born here, among these people, I was a stranger.

III

This landscape, these people! Silver birches
  With polished trunks chalked around a chestnut.
  All is fall-of-night still. No thrush reaches
  Into the earth for worms, nor pulls at the root
  Of a crocus. Dogs have led their masters home.
I stroll, head bowed, hearing only the sound of loam[6]

---

[4]**epics**   stories of a long journey or series of events
[5]**monologue**   a long speech or story told by one person
[6]**loam**   a good-quality soil

At my heel's touch. Now I am intimate
  With England; we meet, secret as lovers.
  I pluck leaves and speak into the air's mouth;
  As a woman's hair, I deck with flowers
  The willow's branches; I sit by the pond,
My eyes are stars in its stillness; as with a wand,

I stir the water with a finger until
  It tosses waves, until countries appear
  From its dark bed: the road from Putney Hill
  Runs across oceans into the harbour
  Of Bombay. To this country I have come.
Stranger or an inhabitant, this is my home.

Further reading

If you enjoyed this poem, two collections that provide insight into other cultures, and in which there are poems about living or arriving in the UK, are *Trade Winds: Poetry in English from Different Cultures* (Longman, 1990) and *Free My Mind: An Anthology of Black and Asian Poetry* (Puffin Books, 1995).

Entering the City

by Tony Connor

Born in Manchester in 1930, Tony Connor has written both poetry
and plays. Here, he describes a train journey returning to his home
town, and the differing emotions he feels.

The city lies ahead. The vale
is cluttering as the train speeds through.
Hacked woods fall back. The scoop and swell
of cooling towers swing into view.

Acres of clinker,[1] slag-heaps,[2] roads
where lorries rev and tip all night,
railway sidings, broken sheds
brutally bare in arc-light,[3]

summon me to a present far
from Pericles's Athens, Caesar's Rome,[4]
to follow again the river's scar
squirming beneath detergent foam.[5]

I close my book, and rub the glass:
a glance ambiguously dark
entertains briefly scrap-yards, rows
of houses, and a treeless park,

---

[1] **clinker**   a stony residue left over after coal is burnt
[2] **slag-heaps**   piles of waste material from an industrial or mining site
[3] **arc-light**   a very strong, bright light, often used at night on industrial sites
  or sports fields
[4] **Pericles's Athens, Caesar's Rome**   Pericles (Greek) and Caesar (Roman)
  lived in times past, thousands of years ago
[5] **detergent foam**   residue or scum left on the surface of water following
  industrial activity, usually polluting the water

like passing thoughts. Across my head
sundry familiar and strange
denizens[6] of the city tread
vistas I would, and would not, change.

Birth-place and home! The diesel's whine
flattens. Excited and defiled
once more, I heave the window down
and thrust my head out like a child.

Further reading

Other poets who have written about life in the North of England
include Tony Harrison and Simon Armitage. Try the latter's prose
account *All Points North* (Penguin, 1999) or his poetry, *Selected Poems*
(Faber and Faber, 2001).

---

[6]**denizens**   anything foreign: could be a person, animal, plant, even a word

A Journey Back to My Hostage Hell

by Brian Keenan

In 1986, Brian Keenan was working in Beirut in Lebanon as a teacher at the American University when he was abducted by Islamist extremists. He was held for four years, much of the time in solitary confinement, before finally being freed in 1990. He wrote an award-winning account of his time in captivity called *An Evil Cradling*. However, he had not returned to Beirut since his liberation. Here, he describes his feelings and experiences 17 years later when he finally goes back.

Through the window, Lebanon was rising up to meet me. I didn't know what I was feeling except that my stomach was empty – yet I had eaten an excellent lunch only an hour ago.

Outside the porthole I watched the Legoland sprawl[1] of ochre-coloured apartment blocks that climb up the hillsides in complete disorder. I remembered that in Lebanon there was no such thing as planning laws. Indeed, in the Beirut that I had last visited, there was no such thing as law, full stop. Everybody made and upheld their own and murdered any transgressors without question.

My mind flashed back to the Beirut of 17 years ago. The din of the place then was deafening, with cars careering around like souped-up dodgems. Street vendors had turned the shopping areas into an open-air market. The stallholders screamed out their wares; people spoke with wild gesticulations, almost shouting to be heard.

Guns of all sizes were everywhere. You could buy a Kalashnikov[2] for $25 but the magazine to go with it cost more. Every man had a pistol tucked into the waistband of his

---

[1]**Legoland sprawl**   Lego is children's brightly coloured building blocks in regular shapes

[2]**Kalashnikov**   a type of Russian gun

trousers at the small of his back, with an ammunition clip bulging in his pocket.

The seatbelt light flashed above my head and the captain's voice intoned the familiar phrase. 'Enjoy your stay.' I smiled to myself, remembering my last visit.

The Beirut I had lived in two decades ago was a city on the edge. Anxiety, stress and suspicion had reduced it to a macabre fantasy land that was psychotic and almost para-normal. People took refuge in tribal and religious loyalties, not out of conviction but because you had to belong somewhere. Not belonging, not believing, not carrying a gun in a city that was imploding[3] by the hour meant that you could fall through the cracks and disappear suddenly and for no reason.

At night the city was a morgue.[4] A no-go land where only the huge population of stray cats and lonely fools walked the streets. There were no street lights. Strangers never took taxis in case they never reached their destination.

Memories were coming back to me as fast as the ground was flying up to meet me. I remembered the intense watchfulness. Even if you entered into a friendly conversation with someone you knew, it was never an open exchange. It was a veneer[5] behind which the person was scrutinising you and withholding his thoughts.

Someone told me once that you didn't measure the city in square miles but rather the number of dead in any cubic foot. The cubic-foot measure puzzled me at first; but as I looked out on the clutter of apartment blocks, I remembered what it meant. When you have finished killing on the first floor, you move up to the next. One cube after another.

When you absorbed the devastation, street after street, mile after mile, the city looked nothing like a city then. It was like a skull with a great, gaping mouthful of hollow, rotten teeth.

---

[3]**imploding**   bursting inward
[4]**morgue**   a place where dead people are kept before burial or cremation
[5]**veneer**   a thin surface covering

That's what I had left 17 years ago – but what was I coming back to?

I knew that, over the years, the city had renewed itself, rising phoenix[6]-like out of the ashes of civil war. But in the past year the Israeli military machine had reduced the southern suburbs and several villages to mounds of rubble.

Whatever anxieties I had, walking into the arrivals lounge soon dispelled them. Everyone was dressed in gaily coloured clothes. Some had balloons on the end of strings; others had bunches of flowers; many of the young men had both bunches of flowers and boxes of chocolates. Kids jumped up and down excitedly and people waved scarves and arms at new arrivals. The scene looked to me as though someone had opened a giant box of Liquorice Allsorts and sprinkled them with great abandon at the arrivals gate.

Obviously none of this was for me, even if I relished it. It was certainly a far remove from the dimly lit airport I last saw, full of silent men staring at everyone. Each one of them had carried a firearm of some description – but now there wasn't a gun in sight.

The Lebanese have a saying that 'the guest is a gift from God'. I thought about that as I caught a taxi into the city. Although there were no flowers or chocolates or balloons or embraces for me, I was already beginning to feel very much at home. The hunger pangs had miraculously disappeared.

For the next few days I walked around the streets of the Hamra area, with my feet hardly touching the ground. The street vendors and their stalls had gone. Incredibly, the bedlam of the traffic, with horns permanently depressed, had reduced in volume by several decibels. Nor were people screaming their conversations at one another. Instead, they retreated to trendy cafe bars, where they played chess or backgammon and conversed with an air of good-natured languor[7] or passionate engagement.

---

[6]**phoenix**   a mythical bird that would periodically burst into flames, then be re-created with renewed youth

[7]**languor**   quiet, laid-back, easy-going

I loved these places. There was a buzz and ease about them which made me feel like a regular as I listened to conversations moving effortlessly from Arabic to English or French. I looked at the young people around me and thought of my students at the university where I had taught. I wondered where they had gone and if any of them had not survived the Israeli air raids.

The university has survived, as has most of Beirut – apart from the southern suburbs, which have a postcatastrophe appearance about them. Dahiya, the worst-hit area, had been exclusively Hezbollah[8] territory – a no-go area for outsiders.

When I drove into part of it with a Lebanese driver, I could feel waves of repulsion coming out of the rubble of half-demolished apartments. Some people were still living in makeshift accommodation. Their eyes followed our car with suspicion. 'Let's leave,' I said, unable to bear the unspoken accusation that I felt was being thrown at us.

The word 'holocaust'[9] entered my head as I looked back at the devastation. History is supposed to tell us what not to repeat – but it seems that for the Israeli military machine, the needle has got stuck.

After that, walking through the gates of the American University was like walking into paradise. I recognised immediately every brick and bush of its tranquil campus and was almost sick with longing. I imagined that I could hear the cheery voices of my long-gone students greeting me. 'Good morning, Mr Brian,' or 'Bye, Mr Brian. See you tomorrow.'

I had loved this place, loved my job here and loved my students. I felt I belonged here. As I stood watching some young people saunter easily through the grounds, I felt pangs of anger and regret about what had happened so long ago, which had stolen from me all the pleasurable years I might have spent here.

---

[8]**Hezbollah**   an extreme Islamist group
[9]**holocaust**   large-scale destruction; usually refers to the massacre of Jews, and some other minority groups, during World War II

I sat on a bench near the library and recalled the faces of my happy, chirpy students. There was a running track on campus where I used to go jogging every Saturday morning. Sometimes a few of my students would be there, sitting on the bleachers.[10] They would jeer at me good-naturedly: 'Too slow, old man' and 'Maybe we can get you a wheelchair from the infirmary.' I remembered their panic and concern when I feigned a sudden heart attack.

Without thinking, I quietly removed the visitor's badge I had been given at the porter's lodge. I didn't want to be a visitor here.

It was three weeks before term-time, but the grounds were already buzzing with students. I stopped a few and asked if the running track was still there. They looked at me puzzled for a moment. 'You have been here before?' one of them asked. I explained that I had taught here 20 years ago.

'That was during the war. What was that like?' They were genuinely curious.

'I survived,' I said, trying to avoid going into any detail, and then quickly asked them about their own plans for the future.

Eventually the conversation got back to what the Lebanese call 'the Wada', which means the current situation. The Wada has a habit of coming up in every conversation no matter whom it's with or how it starts.

'No, there will never be another civil war,' they assured me, but these young people, like everyone else I spoke to, were acutely aware that anything that happens in the wider Middle East has a habit of coming home to roost in Lebanon. Everyone was anxious about the future. Not because of a kind of cultural pessimism, nor because of the cyclical violence that seems to be rooted in local politics. They all insisted that something much bigger was on the horizon.

One afternoon I visited my old Turkish villa, where the daughter of the man I had originally rented it from was now

---

[10]**bleachers**   American term for a set of outdoor wooden benches arranged in tiers

living. If going to the university had made me wistful, being at home in my villa stirred up the same emotion in double measure. I sat on the veranda, where I used to read and drink fine Lebanese wine or Turkish coffee each evening. Surrounded by a classical Islamic garden, I was in my own idyllic little world. But it was mine no longer and I was sadder to leave it than I cared to admit.

Even the memory of my kidnapping, which had happened just outside its gate, had not dispelled the enchantment.

Further reading

Brian Keenan was one of several hostages who were taken at about the same time and remained in captivity in the Lebanon for several years. Keenan's own account, *An Evil Cradling* (Vintage, 1993), tells this story, but it is also worth looking at what was written by two of the men held at the same time – and sometimes in the same place – as him. Read Terry Waite's *Taken on Trust* (Coronet, 1994) and *Some Other Rainbow* (Corgi, 1994) by John McCarthy (held with Keenan) and John's then partner Jill Morrell who campaigned tirelessly for their release.

Activities

Spilled Water

Before you read

1   Imagine you were visiting for the first time a city miles away from the village you grew up in. Talk with a partner about how you would feel if you were on your own. Would you talk with people, or keep to yourself? Now compare this with how you might feel and behave if you went with a large group of friends – how would you behave differently?

What's it about?

2   Look at the first paragraph. How are the outskirts of the town different from the shopping area? Find two descriptions of each and note them down, underlining the words or phrases that show the contrast between the two.

3   During her visit to the shopping area, Lu Si-yan does three main things that she wouldn't normally be able to do whilst working at the factory. List these things: what are they – and which of them cost her money?

4   Lu Si-yan compares the two towns she had previously visited with this one: the one she had visited with her father was 'colourful and bustling'. How does she describe the one Mrs Chen took her to, and how is this place different from that? Write a paragraph, noting down the two descriptive phrases she uses.

Thinking about the text

5   What do we learn about Lu Si-yan's situation? Discuss with a partner:
   ● Has she been here before? How do we know?
   ● How does she get on with her fellow workers?
   ● How does she feel about being away from her village?

6   Imagine that Lu Si-yan saves enough money to leave the factory and return to her tiny village. How will she react to the place where she grew up as a child, and where everyone is a farmer or farmer's daughter? Write a diary entry from her point of view in which she recounts her return.

No Turning Back

Before you read

1   Have you come across homeless children on the streets begging when you have visited towns or cities? In your groups discuss how you felt and whether you were sympathetic to their situation. Talk about how young people end up being homeless, and the difficulties they face on the streets.

What's it about?

2   The writer describes how Sipho and his friends are very much outsiders in the city, and face danger or problems in different forms. Discuss with a partner what threats he and his friends face in this extract.

3   There are a number of vivid descriptions in the extract. Choose one of the following and then make notes saying what you think it adds to the extract in terms of atmosphere or the story itself:
   * The description of the carved rhino and elephant on the market stall
   * The children in school uniform in the car
   * The walk down the hill away from the shops.

Thinking about the text

4   How safe do you think Sipho is in the city? Think about the positive and negative points about his life, and then write 1–2 paragraphs explaining your viewpoint.

5   Jabu makes the point at the end of the extract that he, Sipho and the others are different from the *tsotsis*. In what ways?

6   Imagine that when the children in the car saw Sipho, they wound down the window and started speaking to him. Write a short script in which they speak with Sipho. Use the beginning provided below if you wish.
   Scene: At the traffic lights.
   Two children, Boy and Girl, in a car poke their tongues out at Sipho. He pokes his out in return:

   Boy: *(surprised)*   Mama! Look at that boy.

   Mother: Take no notice.

   Girl: *(winding down window)*   I want to talk to him . . .

The Ruined Maid

Before you read

1   Thomas Hardy wrote a poem called *Wessex Heights*. Do an Internet search for it and when you find it read verses 3 and 4. What seems to be his attitude to the town? Does he like or dislike it, do you think?

2   Check that you are clear about the difference between 'accent' and 'dialect' by looking in a dictionary or on the Internet. Thomas Hardy came from Dorset – have a look at the website http://www.dorsetshire.com and click on 'Dorset dialect' to find out more.

What's it about?

3   The poem is in the form of a dialogue. With a partner go through the text and decide *who* is speaking each line, and then prepare a rehearsed reading of it. Think carefully about the way the two women – the main speaker, and 'Melia – say their lines. Does one have more of a Dorset accent than the other?

4   The poem contrasts 'Melia's life in town with the life she left behind in the countryside. Copy out the grid below and make notes comparing the changes in her appearance and speech.

	Countryside (old life)	Town (new life)
Clothing		
Work and wealth		
Hands and face		
Language (way of speaking)		

Thinking about the text

5   The poem follows a strong rhythm and rhyme scheme. Note down:
   - how it is organised (for example, lines 1 and 2 rhyme, and lines 3 and 4)
   - what you notice about all the 3rd and 4th lines of each verse
   - whether you think the regular rhythm and rhyme match the subject matter.

6   Write your own simple dialogue poem of two verses between someone working in a town and someone in the countryside. Try to copy a similar rhythm, and contrast their ways of life.

Estates

Before you read

1 Do you live on an estate, or know friends who live on one? What is the name of the estate and how would you describe it? What would be your definition of an estate? Write it down and then compare it with a partner's – do you agree?

What's it about?

2 What word or phrase is the one that the writer connects most closely with the estate her parents live on, do you think? Note it down and see if you have chosen the same one as other members of your class.

3 Throughout the text, Lynsey Hanley uses several similes to describe the estate, for example saying it's like 'a never-ending maze'. Find the two similes she uses in the two long second and third paragraphs to describe:
   a the flat-roofed houses
   b the fronts of terraced houses.

   Then write a sentence on each saying how effective you think they are. Later in the text there are further similes – can you find these too?

Thinking about the text

4 With a partner discuss what we find out about Lynsey and her family from this extract. For example:
   - Which members of her family still live on the estate?
   - What are their houses like?

5 The writer is returning as an adult to the place she left at 18 years old. Re-read the long paragraph starting 'The estate splashes itself over four pages . . .'. Discuss in your group:
   - What does she remember from her childhood?
   - What things are still the same for the writer?
   - What has changed in the way she reacts to the estate?

6 Imagine you have been asked to deliver a letter to a house on the Wood Estate and get lost. Write a short story describing what happens to you, and how you feel being lost on the estate. Base your descriptions of the estate on what you have read in the extract.

A Home from Home

Before you read

1   Have you seen pictures of the Statue of Liberty or seen it in real life? Discuss with a partner: why do you think it is seen as a symbol of America? What message do you think it sends out to people arriving by sea in New York?

What's it about?

2   Where can the poem by Emma Lazarus be found? Re-read the poem itself and write 1–2 paragraphs about the poem answering these questions:
   ● Who seems to be speaking – and what is the message of the poem?
   ● Is it a warning, a welcome . . . or something else?

3   The second part of the text deals with a 'little corner of Manhattan' where many immigrants once lived and where a house is preserved as a museum. What do we learn about 97 Orchard Street – the building itself, and the people who lived there? Discuss in your group these questions and make notes about what you have found out.

Thinking about the text

4   In a group, discuss the text as a whole. Do you think it presents a positive or negative image of immigration? What evidence can you find from the text to support your viewpoint?

5   There are three extracts from other texts quoted in George Alagiah's piece. One is lines from a poem on the Statue of Liberty; the second is the nationalistic song, 'God Bless America'; and the third is a song from *West Side Story*. Copy the grid below, and make notes on the different views about America given in each row.

Text	View of America?
Emma Lazarus's poem	
'God Bless America'	
'America' (song from *West Side Story*)	

6   Imagine you are Nathalie Gumpertz living at 97 Orchard Street in 1874 – just after your husband has disappeared. Describe your typical day as a dressmaker, living with your children in the three-roomed apartment.

This Landscape, These People

Before you read

1 In a small group, discuss whether you know anyone who has come to the UK from a country with a very different climate. How do you think they felt on arrival and what major differences do you think they noticed?

2 Looking at the title of the poem, what does it suggest about the poet's attitude to living in England?

What's it about?

3 How long has the poet been in England when he writes the poem?

4 Zulfikar Ghose contrasts the landscape of England with his time in India. Looking at the first four verses, work with a partner to identify descriptions of the two places. Discuss in what ways they are different. Does one seem more attractive than the other?

5 Working on your own, work out the rhyme structure of each verse. Then make notes on these questions:
   ● Does the poet use perfect rhymes all the time, or are they sometimes half-rhymes?
   ● Why does he divide the poem into two halves?

Thinking about the text

6 The poet uses a number of powerful similes and metaphors to describe England, for example saying 'England for me / Is an exhibit within a glass case'. Can you find the other image he uses in this verse? Write 2–3 sentences saying what you think it – and the 'glass case' metaphor – tell us about his feelings for England.

7 Re-read the last two lines of the poem. In a group discuss the poem as a whole and talk about how you think the poet feels about England by the end of the poem.

8 Write your own two-verse poem of six lines each, called 'Coming to England'. Imagine you have arrived from a country with a very different climate.
   a In the first verse describe living in an English town or city.
   b In the second verse describe the place you have just left.

Entering the City

Before you read

1   Have you ever taken a train journey into a town or city from the countryside? Imagine you are on that train now. Jot down 5–10 lines or sentences in which you write what you see as you approach the city and enter it. You could start:
Green fields with cows grazing give way to roads . . .

What's it about?

2   The poem itself describes the poet's journey, what he's doing and what he sees through the train window. Discuss with a partner:
   ● How does the first line set the scene and the time?
   ● What has he been doing on the train until the fourth stanza?
   ● What does he do right at the end of the journey?

3   Tony Connor paints a vivid picture of the city. Make a list of the places and things he sees (e.g. 'cooling towers') once he leaves the countryside. Write a short account in which you explain whether it is an attractive picture he paints, or not – and give your reasons.

4   There is quite a regular rhyme scheme to the poem, with lines 2 and 4 of each stanza ending in perfect rhymes, and lines 1 and 3 usually rhyming too. Usually such a strong rhyme scheme might not fit a 'serious' poem. Discuss with a partner: how is the rhythm broken up in other ways (think about where the sentences end)?

Thinking about the text

5   Write a longer analysis of the poem in which you explore how Tony Connor feels about entering the city. (Draw on your original analysis for activity 3.)

6   Turn your notes from activity 1 into a poem or a short descriptive first-person account in which you arrive in a city by train. Make sure you:
   ● use vivid descriptions of what you can see from your window, especially noun phrases (e.g. 'treeless park')
   ● include how you feel about the place you are travelling to (is it a place you have been to before, a childhood home, a new city?).

A Journey Back to My Hostage Hell

Before you read

1   Brian Keenan's imprisonment made national and international headlines for many years in the mid to late 1980s. Do some basic research into what happened and find out about who else was kidnapped at the same time, and what happened to them. Write this up as a short encyclopaedia entry, with:
- heading/title
- a box for an image (suggest one)
- key information written in prose
- box of bullet-point key facts.

What's it about?

2   The extract begins with Keenan arriving by plane in Lebanon. At this point he remembers Beirut when he last visited it. On your own, read from the beginning down to 'That's what I had left 17 years ago – but what was I coming back to?' Then, make notes about the 'old' Beirut – what it looked like, how people behaved, the dangers people faced.

3   Keenan ends this section with a very powerful metaphor based on a skull. Copy out the metaphor, and then write a sentence or two saying how effective you think it is, and why Keenan chooses it to describe Beirut at that time.

4   There are a lot of contrasts and changes in the new Beirut. With a partner, go through the text and find the ones that are most notable. Discuss how Keenan feels about these changes – for example, has everything improved?

Thinking about the text

5   Re-read the section from when Keenan goes back to the American University to '. . . something much bigger was on the horizon'. Discuss in a group:
- How does Brian Keenan react to being back in the university?
- What do the students he meets feel about the future for Beirut?

6   Imagine you are a student at the American University and you write a letter home to your parents in the UK who are worried about your safety. Describe Beirut as you see it, and your feelings about living there.

Compare and contrast

1   Write a short essay in which you compare the similar and different experiences of people returning to a town or city they have been away from for a while. You might like to look at:
    - *Entering the City*
    - *A Journey Back to My Hostage Hell*
    - *Estates.*

2   In order of priority, create a list of the places mentioned in this section, with the one you would most like to visit at the top, and the least likely at the bottom. Alongside each place add a note saying *why* you would like to visit it.

3   Nearly all the writers in this section are describing situations when people leave home to visit, or revisit, a city. In your group, choose three volunteers to take on the roles of people from the texts (e.g. Sipho, the poet in *This Landscape*, and Brian Keenan). The rest of your group can prepare questions to ask them about their experiences in the different cities. Then, run a 'hot-seating' session in which they talk about what happened to them and how they felt. If you wish you could join up with other groups to create a wider discussion and question/answer session.

4   Imagine you have been given the job of designing a monument, sculpture etc. which is going to be placed at an airport in the UK. Draw or describe what the sculpture would look like and suggest any words or message that might be included on it. Think about, or research, similar structures, like the Angel of the North near Newcastle, or the Statue of Liberty.

5   Tony Connor writes in verse to describe returning to the city of his childhood; Lynsey Hanley writes in non-fiction prose. Write about the advantages and disadvantages of using these two forms of writing to describe your feelings, memories and information about your childhood.

3 Penthouse and pavement

This section of the book focuses on the wide contrasts between the experiences of people living in the same city, from the super-rich of São Paulo to the homeless children living beside railway tracks in India. It describes how cities are changing, but also how others are left behind, and shows that this is not a new thing, as the extracts from D. H. Lawrence's poem and Dickens's account of London show. Finally, Jon McGregor's more optimistic piece provides a wide-sweeping picture of a city with all its various colours, sounds and movements.

Activities

1   There has been a popular programme on television called *The Secret Millionaire*. In it, a millionaire businessman or woman lives in a very poor area of the UK pretending to be someone else who hasn't got much money. Over two weeks they try to get to know the area and

decide at the end who they can help by giving money to. Write a short story in which you are a 'secret millionaire'; you can do it as a series of diary entries if you wish, saying who you meet, what you find out and who you are going to help.

2   Are there any disadvantages to being very, very wealthy? As a class, conduct a debate with one side arguing: 'Being rich is the loneliest thing in the world', while the other argues against it.

3   Design your own luxury bedroom. It must be in the same flat or house you live in now, but it can have anything you want in it.
   ● Draw a plan of your room, or a drawing, labelled with the furniture and other objects you would have (if any).
   ● Write an explanation of your choices underneath.

4   Homelessness remains a huge problem around the UK and the world in general. How would you address the problem? In groups, discuss the issue and make a list of five key ideas you would propose to deal with it. Then present your ideas to another group who will take on the role of a government advisory panel. It is their job to decide if any of your ideas are worthwhile. Your group should be aware that:
   ● anything you suggest that costs money will have to be paid for somehow by government or through some other means
   ● ideas can be inventive, but must be practical too.

The Railway Children

by Raekha Prasad

> This article is taken from the ActionAid charity's magazine, *Common Cause*, which is sent out to people who give to the charity. Taking its title from E. E. Nesbit's famous children's novel of the same name, the article describes a project that is helping homeless children living on station platforms in India's cities return to their families.

Rohit Thakur leans against a motorbike parked in the chaotic entrance to Bhopal railway station, imitating the swagger of a brawny Bollywood[1] star. But the 12-year-old looks nothing like an action hero. He is small for his age, his clothes are grubby and frayed, and his feet are bare. Far from being invincible,[2] he is covered in scars.

The railway station is Rohit's home and his playground. By day he sweeps out the train carriages that pull up from all over India to Madhya Pradesh's capital and begs from passengers. Often, he will lunch on the leftover food thrown out from the 2.10pm Shatabdi Express, India's fastest and most prestigious train. Most nights he sleeps on the platform with other street children.

It has been four years since Rohit ran away from his alcoholic father, who lives in Ujjain, a town several hours' drive away from Bhopal. He left because his father would beat him up. Now, at the station, he faces violence from a gamut of men. Officers from the Railway Protection Force and the General Railway Police, petty shopkeepers, rickshaw drivers and older boys see the children as easy targets. Beatings and sexual abuse are all too common.

'When we come to the platform and talk to him, then Rohit agrees to get off the platform and come to our shelter.

---

[1]**Bollywood**   the Indian equivalent of Hollywood, based in Mumbai (which was formerly known as Bombay)
[2]**invincible**   unconquerable, cannot be defeated

But after two days he comes back to the station again,' says Dilip Kudape, programme coordinator of a project working to rehabilitate[3] platform children, supported by ActionAid.

When the boy is asked why, he cups his hand over his mouth and inhales deeply by way of explanation. 'I have to have solution[4] and they don't allow it there,' he says. Like so many of the kids in the station, Rohit is addicted to the fumes of a solution used to fix punctures. Of the 100 rupees (£1.20) he earns a day, 70% is spent on his fix.

More than 11 million children live on India's streets – the single largest number of street kids in the world. What makes most children run is violence and poverty and almost all runaways take the rail route out. When they get down at a station, many never manage to leave the platform.

---

[3]**rehabilitate**   restore to normal life
[4]**solution**   glue, of the type used for glue-sniffing

Newcomers are quickly sniffed out by the gangs and rackets that operate from the junctions. Boys survive by selling plastic bottles, packets of betel nut and tobacco, sweeping floors, pickpocketing and begging. Runaway girls are vulnerable to pimps[5] and rape. Although the rights of children in India have government protection in principle – it signed the UN convention on the rights of the child in 1992 – in practice the most basic rights of children living in slums, government institutions and street children are routinely violated.

Platform children are stigmatised[6] and labelled as delinquents and criminals by the very railway and police officers who commit physical and sexual assault against them. To better protect the rights of children living on the three busiest platforms in Madhya Pradesh, ActionAid launched Bachpan – meaning 'childhood' in Hindi – and today supports the project's implementation by the National Institute for Women, Child and Youth Development.

The initiative involves outreach[7] workers developing the trust of children dwelling on three platforms: Bhopal, Katni to the east and Itarsi, one of Madhya Pradesh's oldest and most important railway junctions, to the south.

Around 300 runaways a month arrive at the stations. 'We spot newcomers wandering around and approach them and let them know they have support,' explains Kudape. In each location, Bachpan has a 24-hour shelter where platform children can eat, sleep and come and go freely. Since August, the shelters have been funded by the state education department which also provides places in local schools for those children who live there permanently.

Bachpan aims to get children off the platform and into a safe environment. 'We never force them to go back home but encourage them to think about their situation there compared

---

[5]**pimps**   people who live off the earnings of others who offer sex for money
[6]**stigmatised**   seen as unworthy, disgraceful
[7]**outreach**   organisation involved in community welfare

to that of the platform,' Kudape says. 'First of all they tell lies about where they're from because they're scared they'll have to go back. But we accept the things the children say and never accuse them of contradicting their story.'

The project has placed 551 runaways back home since 2005. It has also reduced the number of children under the age of 12 living on the platforms by staff immediately detecting new arrivals and making them aware of the multiple risks they face if they remain sleeping in the station. Bachpan has, in addition, worked to raise the awareness of police and railway officials about the impact of their abuse and harassment of the children.

For those children who are not ready to consider a life away from the platform, Bachpan runs a special camp for 28 boys. In the first week the children are encouraged to have fun, playing cricket and football away from the stress of the stations. By the second week the runaways reflect on what happens to them on the platform.

'They realise that they were beaten by their stepfather but now they're getting beaten up by the police, the shopkeepers and the other kids. They're like small adults and very independent-natured so they think about the disadvantages of this power-lessness,' says Shrirang Dhavale, regional manager of ActionAid.

By the third week, most of the children begin to talk about going home. Project workers begin to contact their families – through local police stations – and invite them to come and meet their runaway. At the last camp, 15 parents of the 28 children on the camp made what were often long journeys to be reunited with their child.

'We had parents and children in tears. We had violent fathers speaking about how they missed their child and the child speaking openly about how scared he is of the violence,' Dhavale recalls. By the end of the camp, every child that went through it had returned home.

Parents are counselled on the impact their violence has had on their child and the local police are made aware that they need to enforce child protection. Project workers also make follow-up calls to those children who return home. Of the 84 children that chose to give their families a second chance after going on the camp, only 5% have returned to the platform. ActionAid plans to extend the project to three more platforms in Madhya Pradesh next year.

Ashu, 13, who ran away from his violent and alcoholic father in his village in the south of Madhya Pradesh, ended up selling plastic bottles, addicted to solution and beaten up by passengers, police officers and vendors[8] at Katni station. He was reunited with his family at the end of a Bachpan residential camp and is now living back in the village and going to school. 'In the closing ceremony of the camp I suddenly saw my father approaching me,' he says. 'I was surprised and thrilled to see him. He hugged me and promised me that he will never beat me again.'

Further reading

The title for this article is an ironic reference to the more innocent children's world of E. E. Nesbit's classic tale *The Railway Children*, also made into a well-loved film. For a broader view of an Indian city, try *Maximum City: Bombay Lost and Found* by Suketu Mehta (Headline Review, 2005).

---

[8] **vendors**   street sellers

São Paulo – City of the Future

by Rory Carroll

São Paulo is the largest city in Brazil, with a population of over 11 million people, and represents both the increasing modernisation of Brazil's cities, and the remaining problems that face the millions who still live in poverty. In this article, Rory Carroll takes a helicopter ride over the city and explores the contrasts between rich and poor.

The pilot flicks the ignition and the blades scythe the air, slowly at first, then a blur, until the helicopter judders and begins to lift. It surges forward, past the edge of the helipad, and in a blink the ground beneath us drops more than 300 feet.

We have just flown off the roof of Banco Safra, a 26-storey São Paulo skyscraper about the height of Big Ben, and in this bubble of glass and steel it is a stomach-tightening experience.

Well, for a first-timer it is. For Gilberto Kassab, the city's mayor, it is a banality.[1] He does this almost daily, a routine so well-established he does not flinch as the helicopter, a municipal-owned aircraft named Eagle 3, swoops down Avenida Paulista.

A picture of tranquillity, Kassab gazes over the skyline. The city stretches into the horizon, a concentration of humanity so vast, so chaotic, that he travels by air to do his rounds. 'It's big,' he says with some understatement. 'Really big.'

This morning's journey – to inaugurate[2] a new school on the periphery – yields an aerial snapshot of Brazil's commercial and financial capital. It is an instructive ride.

Avenida Paulista, the city's main drag, could pass for Manhattan. The headquarters of banks and corporate giants form concrete canyons and the fast-moving specks on the pavements show an army of worker ants in a hurry.

---

[1]**banality**   dull normality
[2]**inaugurate**   first open for public use

The helicopter banks west over the Pinheiros river, and through a haze of pollution it skims over apartment blocks and six-lane motorways jammed with traffic. The skyscrapers disappear and there is a swathe of green, the jockey club, then mansions with gardens and swimming pools. Morumbi, the swankiest district.

The glimpse of privilege swiftly gives way to a lower-middle class area where houses contract and cluster together. As we approach the periphery, it turns into a slum. An endless vista of packed, jumbled brick dwellings sheeted with tin roofs.

The helicopter touches down in Guaianases, a shantytown. The 15-mile journey lasted just 10 minutes but we have landed in a different world, as if we had swapped Canary Wharf for Kampala.[3] Broken and potholed roads, uncollected rubbish abuzz with flies, legions of children without proper schooling or health care.

'Our inequality is one of the greatest in the world,' says Kassab. 'But it's narrowing. Things are getting better.' The school, a sturdy two-storey building with decent plumbing, is part of a wider effort to bridge the gap between rich and poor, he says.

After decades of neglect, state services, not least law and order, are reaching the periphery where most Paulistas live.

After painful adjustments in the 1990s, Brazil's economy is purring. A credit boom is helping to drive record car sales, bank profits and stock exchange gains. Foreign direct investment is flooding in and real incomes are rising. Growth last year reached 5%.

As ever it is São Paulo, whose 11m inhabitants are considered workaholics[4] by the rest of Brazil, that is setting the pace. The city dominates financial services, prompting the cliché that Rio does carnival, Brasilia does politics and Sampa, as it is widely

---

[3]**Kampala**   the capital of Uganda, a country in Africa
[4]**workaholics**   people who can't stop working; they appear to be addicted
   to it

known, does money. The state of São Paulo, long a magnet for migrants from the north-east, has 40 million inhabitants and hosts booming industries such as car and plane manufacturing.

The question is to what extent this shiny, successful São Paulo is connecting with the squalid shantytowns. To answer that requires another trip from the centre to the periphery, but this time at ground level.

An obvious starting point is the main stock exchange, Bovespa. It soared 73% last year, making it a market darling and symbol of Brazil's bid to become a Latin tiger.[5] Values have tumbled since January, partly because of global conditions, but a proposed merger with the BM&F, Brazil's main futures exchange, has rekindled bullishness.[6] 'For the first time people have the confidence to plan ahead, to invest in the long term, to buy,' says Gilberto Mifano, Bovespa's chief executive.

Surging production of ethanol, the biofuel derived from sugar cane, has heightened the giddy atmosphere. The revival of cane as an economic force brings São Paulo full circle since it was founded originally as a series of sugar plantations before giving way to coffee in the 19th century and industry in the 20th.

Now the crop is again making people rich. And merry. Visit the Skybar, or any number of designer watering holes around the leafy Jardins area, and you see people knocking back caipirinhas and other sugar cane-derived cocktails like there was no tomorrow. Conspicuous consumption[7] is visible in the restaurants, packed every night, as well as the sports cars and 4 × 4s, which accounted for many of the 2.5m vehicles sold last year, a 28% rise from 2006.

That boom has compounded horrendous traffic jams, which make commuting torture. For the rich, as ever, there is a

---

[5]**Latin tiger**   a South American country whose economy developed very quickly

[6]**bullishness**   in economic terms, taking aggressive risks, causing a rise in stock market prices

[7]**conspicuous consumption**   visible purchasing by people of goods and services

way out: helicopters. São Paulo has 462 private helicopters, second only to New York, and for a few thousand dollars an hour they can zip you across the city. Air traffic has grown so fast that the city recently regulated it.

Helicopters are a genuine work tool for executives – or so they insist – but they are also a status symbol. None more so than the one that hangs in the atrium[8] of Daslu, the city's plushest shopping emporium. A shrine to luxury, Daslu has a helipad for clients, of course, but it uses its own helicopter as a sort of mannequin.[9] Draped in cashmere for the launch of the store's winter collection, its next, er, outfit is a closely guarded secret.

'Business just gets better and better. Brazil is going up and we're going up with it,' exults Daniella Lunardelli, a spokeswoman. Staff are dressed in black and white livery to resemble servants and there is a champagne bar to get clients in the mood before a consultant advises on how best to coordinate a £2,800 Balenciaga handbag with £1,000 Tod's shoes and a £4,200 Dolce & Gabbana dress.

Given that the monthly minimum wage is just over £100 and that the city's 8,000-plus homeless people rummage in bins for food, you don't need to be Karl Marx to deplore the blatant materialism of those at the top.

London, Paris and New York have their own shameful juxtapositions of rich and poor, true, but São Paulo's is in a league of its own. The melting pot image of a city that blends all colours into one belies the reality that the blacker you are the likelier you are to be poor, uneducated and jobless.

Paraisopolis, one of the biggest slums, is a vast warren of shabbily built brick homes clinging precariously to a hillside. In the rainy season they have a habit of being swept away in mudslides, burying families alive.

---

[8]**atrium**   central hall or court, often rising through several storeys of a tall building
[9]**mannequin**   model on which clothes are displayed

The higher up the hill the worse homes become. Wooden walls, plastic sheeting roofs, no electricity or running water. Gang-fuelled crime, especially cocaine trafficking, is rife.

The sense of frustration and alienation is palpable. 'Helicopters, ha! It's absurd,' Jose Batista, a wiry 34-year-old community leader, says indignantly. 'The government should be investing in public transport to help us get into town and find work.'

Government-funded houses are being built on the site of cleared shacks but residents suspect it is a plot to create space for a middle class development, not an irrational fear given the experience of some other slums. Government schemes such as Bolsa Familia, a stipend[10] for the poorest, has filled bellies but done nothing to integrate shantytowns into the economy, says Batista. 'Food is good but it's not enough.'

In the absence of state services, the First Capital Command, a powerful, quasi-military criminal gang based in prisons, has funded schooling and health care for some families, says another community activist, Silveiro de Jesus. Gangsters in charge of certain areas are called pilots because they know their way around.

It seems to add up to a tale wearily familiar across Latin America: an economic boom ushers in salad days[11] for the rich and leaves those at the bottom scrambling for crumbs.

Brazil's recovery is too recent to give a definitive verdict but there is reason to think that this time the outcome will be better, notwithstanding the troubles in Paraisopolis.

The decades-long stream of rural migrants to São Paulo has slowed to a relative trickle, giving much-needed breathing space, and better policing has helped cut the state's murder rate by 70% since 1999. Parts of Rio de Janeiro, in contrast, still resemble war zones.

---

[10]**stipend**   a regular allowance
[11]**salad days**   good times

Generous government social spending has pumped money into the slums, including £73m last year in Paraisopolis. A steep fall in inflation has allowed real incomes to rise and low interest rates have extended credit to the poor.

A telling illustration is the breakneck growth of Casas Bahias, a chain of furniture and electric goods stores, which sells to the poor by letting them pay in monthly instalments.

In the past five years its outlets have almost doubled to 560 and annual revenue has soared to £3.6bn. Even more striking – and arguably this is a bellwether[12] – the chain is signing up 2.5m new customers every year, the vast majority from slums. 'We now have 29m customers. The poor are becoming less poor and many are going on to become middle class,' says Michael Klein, the chain's executive director.

That does not mean the chasm between rich and poor will be bridged any time soon. It is too wide for that. It does mean that this vast concentration of humanity, a Latin version of Gotham[13] famous for extremes, may be on its way to becoming, against all the odds, a kinder, gentler place.

Further reading

Rory Carroll is a writer for *The Guardian*. Feature articles such as this one appear in all newspapers. Have a look at the *Daily Express* website and *The Newspaper* (a children's/teens' newspaper – see http://www. thenewspaper.org.uk/), for example, and see if you can find two articles that are not about breaking news that has happened just at this moment, but instead explore an issue or event. What similarities or differences do you notice between them and Carroll's article?

---

[12]**bellwether**   an indicator of future trends
[13]**Gotham**   a nickname for New York, first used in the early 19th century

The Missing

by Andrew O'Hagan

> This extract follows the author as he visits Centrepoint – a refuge
> centre for young people in London. In it, he talks to several people,
> such as Dolly, an old lady living on the streets, Racine, a young
> homeless mother, and Pete McGinlay, who runs the centre. We find
> out some reasons why people who have disappeared on the streets
> are often so difficult to find.

It was already dark, and everything was wet. The old woman
had tea. She motioned to me, and I went over beside her. We
were in the Strand, where she often slept, and she just wanted
to talk a minute. She seemed like she might be suffering from
Alzheimer's,[1] or maybe from amnesia.[2] I didn't know enough
about either – or about her – to tell. But she spoke fast, though
not all of it made sense. She thought she was Dolly. When I
asked her where she'd lived before she said she thought
Stratford or something. Maybe she had sons, four sons, but she
couldn't right remember. I asked the guy in the van, the terse[3]
captain of the soup kitchen, if he could give me more tea for
her. She was sort of laughing and chattering to nowhere. I
asked if people knew where she was. She sniggered, and blew
into the tea. 'Nobody knows, nothing,' she said.

Just off Shaftesbury Avenue, at the beginning of Dean
Street, there's a place called 'Centrepoint: Off the Streets'. It's
not meant for homeless like Dolly (there's other places, emergency night shelters, filled with the old). This one's for young
people in the West End, who do their thing around the streets
there, and who might want to be indoors now and then. The
main room has sofas and bookshelves, and baskets of plums.

---

[1]**Alzheimer's** a form of mental deterioration seen mostly in older people
[2]**amnesia** forgetfulness
[3]**terse** smart and concise

There are heaps of magazines, scatter cushions, and blue table-tops ready to eat off. The London hostels meant for older vagrants – such as Camden Nightshelter, and Bondway in Vauxhall – are basic and dank; they do the job, but are quite grim. Centrepoint is the opposite of that. It's clear that they want to appear more optimistic; the place itself looks stylish and young, clean and hopeful. Radios are playing, board-games are there, and the food is good and hot. A bellyful of laundry was tumbling in the drier as I walked around downstairs. There were separate dormitories for men and women, and everything was scrubbed. Over a bed at the women's end was a coloured advertising poster, announcing the publication of a new Peter Ackroyd novel. It's like an idea of home, a sort of floating homeliness, which (according to the rules) can be enjoyed no more than eight days a month by a homeless youngster.

Those who pass through those rooms are unknown. They will be asked for a first name, an age, and where they come from, but no one who gives a true answer to these small questions is giving anything away. They remain in almost every sense anonymous. They may come only once, they may appear quite regularly and then never again, they may seem always to be somewhere near, they might come and never want to leave. But they keep most of themselves to themselves, and don't get involved in explanations or consequences or follow-throughs. They're secret. That's not to say they won't speak – they will, about most things – but they won't give themselves up, or away, and won't allow details to go from them which are likely to prove useful in the keeping of tabs.[4] Many are decisively lost, always for running away. They just wander, and escape, and keep running, and stay out of it. For some, this is a tacit[5] agreement between them and their sometime guardians. Being a family doesn't suit either side, so they all blow. Sometimes the family changes, or changes its mind, and decides to make a go of it, but often little Racine is gone, and there's to be no finding her then. A lot of the kids I spoke to had no sense of their relatives' worries: they mostly thought people were glad to be rid of them. Some knew themselves to be missing, though most reckoned they'd never been reported as such. Little Racine, the nineteen-year-old mother in the blue Kangol hat, wasn't sure 'they' knew who she was now, but she was still sure about 'them': they were no good; they'd all hurt her; none of them had any right to know of her existence, much less to follow it.

Racine told me she knew loads of young people in her position. She said the streets were full up. She rolled her eyes when I asked her about those pictures of missing people in the *Big Issue*. 'This woman, right, she came up to me. And I'm like, no way, I can't deal with this. She shows me a picture of this missing girl, who's like my friend and that, and she was upset, looking for her daughter, but I just couldn't say anything. I couldn't give her away.' Racine has been missing herself, though she

---

[4]**keeping of tabs**   keeping records up to date
[5]**tacit**   silent, unspoken

recently phoned some old foster parents to tell them she was fine. She was living on the streets while she was pregnant; sitting, she told me, on the steps of Top Shop in Oxford Street, crying, and waiting for something to happen. I asked her what happened then. She took another cigarette.

'What happened?'

'Where did you go to then?'

'I was here, in here, when the waters broke.'

'Here. When was that?'

She twisted the fag from the corner of her mouth, and sniffed. 'Two weeks ago.'

Racine's child was being looked after by Social Services; but she wanted to give it a proper home herself. 'If I could just have a house,' she said, 'and could make it work.'

Pete McGinlay, who runs the project in Dean Street, is a big man with a grizzly beard. He has a nice touch; he is very obviously sympathetic, and careful. He is quick to spot tension or rambling in the young people who come in – including the journalists who come in – and he will bring down the volume, easing things, taking the piss, and just being a bit human and sorting out people's anxieties. You get the impression he may have had a few of his own, but he seems to let the experience, rather than the words, do the talking. He's the opposite of patronizing, the reverse of a boss-pleaser,[6] and he has a fine sense of social history, a soft spot for society, that is all the more engaging for not being dogmatic[7] or at all hectoring.[8] We sat in the afternoon, with giant mugs of tea.

'A lot of the people we see here,' he says, 'haven't got a home to go to. Many are from care, and there's no going back there. The local authority, which is perhaps the biggest mother of them all, says you must go when you are sixteen, and many

---

[6]**boss-pleaser**   someone who tells their superiors what they want to hear in order to make a favourable impression

[7]**dogmatic**   overbearing; stating personal opinions very strongly

[8]**hectoring**   treating another person rudely, in a bullying manner

of them do.' He feels strongly about confidentiality. The Dean Street operation was set up in 1990 under funding rules which differed from the usual ones. Other hostels would ask for information such as your National Insurance number and the like, so that they could make a claim for rent, reimbursement for having put the individual up. The Housing Benefit Office would accept claims only if accompanied by proper identification, such as NI numbers. There is no obligation to give such information at Centrepoint.

'Where do they go from here,' I ask him, 'whereabouts?'

'About forty-two per cent of those who leave here will say they're leaving to go into longer-term accommodation – that could be into a long-term hostel, or a bedsit or flat scheme. They can tell me that, and I can mark it down as a statistic, but nothing will tell me they stayed there the night after telling me. Some will be back again, because the tenancy will not have worked. But, really, I don't have the right to know what people do when they've moved on. I don't really want to know. What you do know is that a large number of those who come here over the years disappear; they're disappearing, and the best thing you can do to maintain your own sanity is to assume that they're doing OK. You can't bear to imagine them out there, in hell, in worse circumstances than what they were in the last time you saw them.'

Centrepoint opened in 1969, and was accommodating young people under thirty, but over the years the average age has gone down and down. There used to be more young people on the streets of London than anywhere else. But now, in the nineties, there is an increasing number who are homeless in, say, the North, who are responding to homeless projects in their own area. It wasn't really possible, before, to be homeless in Liverpool and Glasgow and to have a life spent between day centres and night shelters.

There were vagrants and winos, for sure, but there was no network for young homeless. They would go to London, and be on the streets there, where more and more young people situated themselves, and where many organizations formed around that situation. These days, there is a young homeless problem in every big space in Britain: Oxford has it, and so does Dundee; Birmingham, Cardiff and Gloucester have it too. And there are agencies now, people responding to this explosion in the numbers of youngsters who are homeless in the vicinity of their former homes.

'It's one thing to leave your housing estate and head for Glasgow city centre,' said McGinlay, 'but if you make the bigger jump and go all the way to London, you might just never make it back. You might not. So we had to look towards funding provision in the local areas.'

Further reading

The plight of the homeless on the streets has been depicted in several novels. Robert Swindell's novel *Stone Cold* (Puffin, 1994) provides a twist in that the chapters are told from different perspectives, including that of a serial killer.

The Lost Sewer Children
by Lutaa Badamkhand

This article, taken from the *Independent* newspaper, describes the lives of children living in the remote capital of Outer Mongolia, Ulan Bator. But these are no ordinary children: they are homeless ones who have to face temperatures on the streets as low as –52 degrees, and as a result seek shelter in the sewers beneath the city.

Outside the window, a blizzard is sweeping across the frozen landscape, driving the temperature to −25 °C. Inside, about two dozen children whose homes are normally in the sewers beneath the streets of Ulan Bator, the capital of Outer Mongolia, find a temporary refuge from the cold, violence and uncertainties of the city.

More than 3,000 children live on the streets here, where temperatures can fall as low as −52 °C. They have been forced out of their family homes by poverty, violent parents or hunger.

They beg, steal, dig through piles of rubbish or wander ice-covered streets to find the wherewithal to survive the perishing winter in this land-locked country sandwiched between Russia and China. But inside the shelter, run by Save the Children UK, one of the three charities in this year's *Independent* Christmas Appeal, they can find some respite from all that. In the warm atmosphere of the charity's sanctuary, they can get a bowl of hot soup, wash, clean their clothes, watch television and even attend art or language classes.

'It is very good to be here,' said one 14-year-old girl, Davaajargal. She was among three teenagers selected to be trained to teach English to other street children at the shelter. 'Today we will meet our English-language teacher and decide on how we will give our first lesson,' she added excitedly.

The crisis of children on the streets was prompted by the collapse of Communism,[1] which sent the economy of the

---

[1]**Communism**   a political system in which all things in society are owned by everyone and each person is paid and works according to his or her needs

former Soviet republic into deep crisis. Most Mongolian factories shut and as much as a third of the 2.4 million population
descended swiftly into poverty, with a further 50 per cent living
on the brink of subsistence.[2] The former centralised social welfare system was unable to cope.

But that was not all. The land is prone to a natural disaster
known as the *dzud*, when sheeted ice formed by melted and
frozen snow prevents animals from grazing on dried grass in
winter. It has struck the country for the past three years, wiping
out as many 3.9 million of the nation's 33 million animals, and
leaving hundreds of nomadic herder[3] families without any
means of subsistence.

This, combined with the sheer pace of social and economic
change, has left thousands of former factory workers and
herders bewildered. The result has been escalating domestic
violence, crime, alcoholism and children driven out onto the
freezing streets.

Children, along with old people and women, have borne
the brunt of the social collapse. Thousands of children moved
on to the streets of the capital in search of the food and cloth-
ing their desperate parents were simply unable to provide.

Bolormaa Nordov, the head of the Mongolian National
Child Rights Centre, says: 'The social changes of the Nineties
took the government and children's organisations by surprise.
We did not know how to tackle the problem of street children,
nor did we have enough resources.'

The situation became so grave it came to the attention of the
international community. Seven years ago, Save the Children
stepped in with funds and much-needed expertise. 'Foreign agencies' assistance was very important in helping us to learn how to
deal with the new problems,' Ms Bolormaa said. Over the years,
Save the Children has built a network of seven shelters.

---

[2]**subsistence**   having only just enough to survive, and no more
[3]**nomadic herder**   farmer who moves from one place to another with his
     grazing animals, in order to find food for them

Ya Narangerel, a social worker with the Save the Children shelter in the capital, said: 'Without such shelters street children would have no place to go other than down the manholes[4] to the sewers. Here they can at least shower, wash clothes and find temporary relief from the harsh realities of living on the streets in our cold winter.'

But even with 10 other street shelters run by other non-governmental organisations the situation is still dire. Estimates put the numbers of street children in Outer Mongolia from 3,700 to 4,000, some as young as five.

The problem has been made worse in the past three years by the rapid movement of nomadic herders hit by the *dzud* into the capital and other large towns. The migration, which the UN has called 'a silent crisis' for children, escalated from an average 10,000 each year during 1992–97 to a record high of 25,000 in 2002. Total population of the capital has soared from 600,000 to one million.

Many of those who move in do not have official registration or a place to live or work. Children of migrant families are hence a particularly vulnerable group because they do not have the necessary documents to enrol in school or get medical services.

Today, some 15 per cent of all children do not attend school. Instead, they often work long hours inside and outside the family to contribute to the family income.

Karlo Puskarica, Save the Children's new country director in Mongolia, said: 'They come hoping for a better life . . . but find themselves in even worse conditions, unable to adapt to urban life which requires much more knowledge and many more skills.'

To meet new challenges, Save the Children is launching an initiative to bring government and agencies together around the street children crisis. 'We feel the problem of street children

---

[4]**manholes**   entrances to a city's sewerage system, usually marked by a horizontal metal cover or grille set in the road or pavement

can't be resolved without concerted effort by all,' Mr Puskarica said. 'We will focus on pooling available resources and forming a broad alliance. It is a complex problem, but with the right approach, the problems of street children in Mongolia will be addressed.'

Already life is looking much better for Davaajargal. 'One day I will learn English very well,' the girl said, her eyes sparkling as she watched the snowflakes falling slowly outside the shelter's window.

'And then I will teach it to others.'

Further reading

Stories and accounts of children who live underground occur both within this collection (*Tanglewreck*) and elsewhere, for example in Neil Gaiman's half-fantasy, half-futuristic novel *Neverwhere* (Harper Perennial, 1996) which is also the subject of a BBC series. A moving documentary film from 2001, *Children Underground* (directed by Edet Belzberg), tells the story of children below the streets of Romania's capital, Bucharest.

Little Dorrit

by Charles Dickens

Charles Dickens, one of the most famous English writers, is perhaps best known for his novel *Oliver Twist* and short story *A Christmas Carol*. In both of those, he shows a keen concern for the poor of London. In this extract, taken from another of his novels, Arthur Clennam, who has recently returned from abroad, is about to set out to visit his aged mother – and we get a nightmarish vision of London in the mid-19th century.

It was a Sunday evening in London, gloomy, close, and stale. Maddening church bells of all degrees of dissonance,[1] sharp and flat, cracked and clear, fast and slow, made the brick-and-mortar echoes hideous. Melancholy streets, in a penitential[2] garb of soot, steeped the souls of the people who were condemned to look at them out of windows, in dire despondency. In every thoroughfare, up almost every alley, and down almost every turning, some doleful bell was throbbing, jerking, tolling, as if the Plague were in the city and the dead-carts[3] were going round. Everything was bolted and barred that could by possibility furnish relief to an overworked people. No pictures, no unfamiliar animals, no rare plants or flowers, no natural or artificial wonders of the ancient world – all *taboo*[4] with that enlightened strictness, that the ugly South Sea gods in the British Museum might have supposed themselves at home again. Nothing to see but streets, streets, streets. Nothing to breathe but streets, streets, streets. Nothing to change the brooding mind, or raise it

---

[1] **dissonance**   lack of harmony
[2] **penitential**   here means black, like the garments worn by someone who is punishing themselves by doing a penance
[3] **dead-carts**   carts that took dead people away from the place where they had died
[4] ***taboo***   forbidden; a word from the language of Tonga, an island in the Pacific

up. Nothing for the spent toiler to do, but to compare the monotony of his seventh day with the monotony of his six days, think what a weary life he led, and make the best of it – or the worst, according to the probabilities.

At such a happy time, so propitious[5] to the interests of religion and morality, Mr Arthur Clennam, newly arrived from Marseilles by way of Dover, and by Dover coach the Blue-eyed Maid,[6] sat in the window of a coffee-house on Ludgate Hill. Ten thousand responsible houses surrounded him, frowning as heavily on the streets they composed, as if they were every one inhabited by the ten young men of the Calender's story,[7] who blackened their faces and bemoaned their miseries every night. Fifty thousand lairs surrounded him where people lived so

---

[5]**propitious**   boding well, favourable
[6]**the Blue-eyed Maid**   the name of the horse-drawn stagecoach that ran between London and Dover
[7]**Calender's story**   a reference to a set of stories from *The Arabian Nights*

unwholesomely that fair water put into their crowded rooms on Saturday night, would be corrupt on Sunday morning; albeit my lord, their county member, was amazed that they failed to sleep in company with their butcher's meat. Miles of close wells and pits of houses, where the inhabitants gasped for air, stretched far away towards every point of the compass. Through the heart of the town a deadly sewer ebbed and flowed, in the place of a fine fresh river. What secular want could the million or so of human beings whose daily labour, six days in the week, lay among these Arcadian[8] objects, from the sweet sameness of which they had no escape between the cradle and the grave – what secular want could they possibly have upon their seventh day? Clearly they could want nothing but a stringent policeman.

Mr Arthur Clennam sat in the window of the coffee-house on Ludgate Hill, counting one of the neighbouring bells, making sentences and burdens of songs out of it in spite of himself, and wondering how many sick people it might be the death of in the course of the year. As the hour approached, its changes of measure made it more and more exasperating. At the quarter, it went off into a condition of deadly-lively importunity,[9] urging the populace in a voluble manner to Come to church, Come to church, Come to church! At the ten minutes, it became aware that the congregation would be scanty, and slowly hammered out in low spirits, They *won't* come, they *won't* come, they *won't* come! At the five minutes, it abandoned hope, and shook every house in the neighbourhood for three hundred seconds, with one dismal swing per second, as a groan of despair.

'Thank Heaven!' said Clennam when the hour struck, and the bell stopped.

But its sound had revived a long train of miserable Sundays, and the procession would not stop with the bell, but continued to march on. 'Heaven forgive me,' said he, 'and those who trained me. How I have hated this day!'

---

[8]**Arcadian**   in Ancient Greek literature, Arcadia was an idyllic country paradise
[9]**importunity**   insistent, persistent request or demand

There was the dreary Sunday of his childhood, when he sat with his hands before him, scared out of his senses by a horrible tract[10] which commenced business with the poor child by asking him in its title, why he was going to Perdition? – a piece of curiosity that he really, in a frock and drawers,[11] was not in a condition to satisfy – and which, for the further attraction of his infant mind, had a parenthesis[12] in every other line with some such hiccuping reference as 2 Ep. Thess. c. iii, v. 6 & 7. There was the sleepy Sunday of his boyhood, when, like a military deserter, he was marched to chapel by a picket of teachers three times a day, morally handcuffed to another boy; and when he would willingly have bartered two meals of indigestible sermon for another ounce or two of inferior mutton at his scanty dinner in the flesh. There was the interminable Sunday of his nonage;[13] when his mother, stern of face and unrelenting of heart, would sit all day behind a Bible – bound, like her own construction of it, in the hardest, barest, and straitest boards, with one dinted ornament on the cover like the drag of a chain, and a wrathful sprinkling of red upon the edges of the leaves – as if it, of all books! were a fortification against sweetness of temper, natural affection, and gentle intercourse. There was the resentful Sunday of a little later, when he sat down glowering and glooming through the tardy length of the day, with a sullen sense of injury in his heart, and no more real knowledge of the beneficent history of the New Testament than if he had been bred among idolaters. There was a legion of Sundays, all days of unserviceable bitterness and mortification, slowly passing before him. 'Beg pardon, sir,' said a brisk waiter, rubbing the table. 'Wish see bed-room?'

'Yes. I have just made up my mind to do it.'

---

[10]**tract**   a short religious pamphlet or leaflet
[11]**frock and drawers**   in Victorian times, young boys wore a dress (frock) and long pants (drawers) until they were around six years old
[12]**parenthesis**   literally, an explanation of a word or phrase (often included within brackets)
[13]**nonage**   under age, a legal minor

'Chaymaid!' cried the waiter. 'Gelen box num seven wish see room!'

'Stay!' said Clennam, rousing himself. 'I was not thinking of what I said; I answered mechanically. I am not going to sleep here. I am going home.'

'Deed, sir? Chaymaid! Gelen box num seven, not go sleep here, gome.'

He sat in the same place as the day died, looking at the dull houses opposite, and thinking, if the disembodied spirits of former inhabitants were ever conscious of them, how they must pity themselves for their old places of imprisonment. Sometimes a face would appear behind the dingy glass of a window, and would fade away into the gloom as if it had seen enough of life and had vanished out of it. Presently the rain began to fall in slanting lines between him and those houses, and people began to collect under cover of the public passage opposite, and to look out hopelessly at the sky as the rain dropped thicker and faster. Then wet umbrellas began to appear, draggled skirts, and mud. What the mud had been doing with itself, or where it came from, who could say? But it seemed to collect in a moment, as a crowd will, and in five minutes to have splashed all the sons and daughters of Adam. The lamp-lighter[14] was going his rounds now; and as the fiery jets sprang up under his touch, one might have fancied them astonished at being suffered to introduce any show of brightness into such a dismal scene.

Mr Arthur Clennam took up his hat and buttoned his coat, and walked out. In the country, the rain would have developed a thousand fresh scents, and every drop would have had its bright association with some beautiful form of growth or life. In the city, it developed only foul stale smells, and was a sickly, lukewarm, dirt-stained, wretched addition to the gutters.

---

[14]**lamp-lighter**   in Victorian times, street lights were fuelled by gas and had to be lit individually each evening

He crossed by St Paul's and went down, at a long angle, almost to the water's edge, through some of the crooked and descending streets which lie (and lay more crookedly and closely then) between the river and Cheapside. Passing, now the mouldy hall of some obsolete Worshipful Company, now the illuminated windows of a Congregationless Church that seemed to be waiting for some adventurous Belzoni[15] to dig it out and discover its history; passing silent warehouses and wharves, and here and there a narrow alley leading to the river, where a wretched little bill, FOUND DROWNED, was weeping on the wet wall; he came at last to the house he sought. An old brick house, so dingy as to be all but black, standing by itself within a gateway. Before it, a square court-yard where a shrub or two and a patch of grass were as rank (which is saying much) as the iron railings enclosing them were rusty; behind it, a jumble of roots. It was a double house, with long, narrow, heavily-framed windows. Many years ago, it had it in its mind to slide down sideways; it had been propped up, however, and was leaning on some half-dozen gigantic crutches: which gymnasium for the neighbouring cats, weather-stained, smoke-blackened, and overgrown with weeds, appeared in these latter days to be no very sure reliance.

'Nothing changed,' said the traveller, stopping to look round. 'Dark and miserable as ever. A light in my mother's window, which seems never to have been extinguished since I came home twice a year from school, and dragged my box over this pavement. Well, well, well!'

He went up to the door, which had a projecting canopy in carved work of festooned jack-towels[16] and children's heads with water on the brain, designed after a once-popular monumental pattern, and knocked. A shuffling step was soon heard

---

[15]**Belzoni**   an Italian adventurer and explorer, who lived in the late 18th / early 19th century, famed for his travels and discovery of Egyptian antiquities

[16]**jack-towels**   towels hung on rollers for communal use

on the stone floor of the hall, and the door was opened by an old man, bent and dried, but with keen eyes. He had a candle in his hand, and he held it up for a moment to assist his keen eyes.

'Ah, Mr Arthur?' he said, without any emotion, 'you are come at last? Step in.'

Mr Arthur stepped in and shut the door.

Further reading

This extract from Dickens's novel *Little Dorrit* mirrors similar accounts of the city of London and its poor, whether it's Scrooge's treatment of his family and employees in *A Christmas Carol* or the lives (and deaths) of the poor as described in *Bleak House*.

Embankment at Night, Before the War

by D. H. Lawrence

D. H. Lawrence (1885–1930) is best known for his novels such as
Sons and Lovers and *The Rainbow*, but he was also a poet with a particular interest in animals, about which he wrote with great honesty
and sensitivity. Here, he is equally honest about his contrasting feelings when he meets a homeless woman asleep by the River Thames.

By the river
In the black wet night as the furtive rain slinks down,
Dropping and starting from sleep
Alone on a seat
A woman crouches.

I must go back to her.

I want to give her
Some money. Her hand slips out of the breast of her gown
Asleep. My fingers creep
Carefully over the sweet
Thumb-mound, into the palm's deep pouches.

So, the gift!

God, how she starts!
And looks at me, and looks in the palm of her hand!
And again at me!
I turn and run
Down the Embankment, run for my life.

But why? – why?

Because of my heart's
Beating like sobs, I come to myself, and stand
In the street spilled over splendidly
With wet, flat lights. What I've done
I know not, my soul is in strife.

The touch was on the quick.[1] I want to forget.

Further reading

Many of Lawrence's poems deal with nature and the countryside, and he has an ability to get 'under the skin' of the creatures he describes. Some of his best poems include *Mountain Lion*, *The Mosquito* and *Snake*.

---

[1] **quick**   the poet's sensitive flesh

If Nobody Speaks of Remarkable Things

by Jon McGregor

The final text in this section comprises the opening pages from a novel set in the present day. In it, the writer presents a northern city's life in all its various forms, just before dawn breaks. The story has not really begun – we haven't met the main characters, or found out about the main event that will affect all their lives – but perhaps, after you have read this, you might consider whether it is the city itself that is the main character.

If you listen, you can hear it.

The city, it sings.

If you stand quietly, at the foot of a garden, in the middle of a street, on the roof of a house.

It's clearest at night, when the sound cuts more sharply across the surface of things, when the song reaches out to a place inside you.

It's a wordless song, for the most, but it's a song all the same, and nobody hearing it could doubt what it sings.

And the song sings the loudest when you pick out each note.

The low soothing hum of air-conditioners, fanning out the heat and the smells of shops and cafes and offices across the city, winding up and winding down, long breaths layered upon each other, a lullaby hum for tired streets.

The rush of traffic still cutting across flyovers, even in the dark hours a constant crush of sound, tyres rolling across tarmac and engines rumbling, loose drains and manhole covers clack-clacking like cast-iron castanets.

Road-menders mending, choosing the hours of least interruption, rupturing the cold night air with drills and jack-hammers and pneumatic pumps, hard-sweating beneath the fizzing hiss of floodlights, shouting to each other like drummers in rock bands calling out rhythms, pasting new skin on the veins of the city.

Restless machines in workshops and factories with endless shifts, turning and pumping and steaming and sparking, pressing and rolling and weaving and printing, the hard crash and ring and clatter lifting out of echo-high buildings and sifting into the night, an unaudited product beside the paper and cloth and steel and bread, the packed and the bound and the made.

Lorries reversing, right round the arc of industrial parks, it seems every lorry in town is reversing, backing through gateways, easing up ramps, shrill-calling their presence while forklift trucks gas and prang around them, heaping and stacking and loading.

And all the alarms, calling for help, each district and quarter, each street and estate, each every way you turn has alarms going off, coming on, going off, coming on, a hammered ring like a lightning drum-roll, like a mesmeric bell-toll, the false and the real as loud as each other, crying their needs to the night like an understaffed orphanage, babies waawaa-ing in darkened wards.

Sung sirens, sliding through the streets, streaking blue light from distress, to distress, the slow wail weaving urgency through the darkest of the dark hours, a lament lifted high, held above the rooftops and fading away, lifted high, flashing past, fading away.

And all these things sing constant, the machines and the sirens, the cars blurting hey and rumbling all headlong, the hoots and the shouts and the hums and the crackles, all come together and rouse like a choir, sinking and rising with the turn of the wind, the counter and solo, the harmony humming expecting more voices.

So listen.
Listen, and there is more to hear.
The rattle of a dustbin lid knocked to the floor.
The scrawl and scratch of two hackle-raised cats.

The sudden thundercrash of bottles emptied into crates. The slam-slam of car doors, the changing of gears, the hobbled clip-clop of a slow walk home.

The rippled roll of shutters pulled down on late-night cafes, a crackled voice crying street names for taxis, a loud scream that lingers and cracks into laughter, a bang that might just be an old car backfiring, a callbox calling out for an answer, a treeful of birds tricked into morning, a whistle and a shout and a broken glass, a blare of soft music and a blam of hard beats, a barking and yelling and singing and crying and it all swells up all the rumbles and crashes and bangings and slams, all the noise and the rush and the non-stop wonder of the song of the city you can hear if you listen the song

and it stops

in some rare and sacred dead time, sandwiched between the late sleepers and the early risers, there is a miracle of silence.

Everything has stopped.

And silence drops down from out of the night, into this city, the briefest of silences, like a falter between heartbeats, like a darkness between blinks. Secretly, there is always this moment, an unexpected pause, a hesitation as one day is left behind and a new one begins.

A catch of breath as gasometer lungs begin slow exhalations.

A ring of tinnitus as thermostats interrupt air-conditioning fans. These moments are there, always, but they are rarely noticed and they rarely last longer than a flicker of thought.

We are in that moment now, there is silence and the whole city is still.

The old tall-windowed mills, staggered across the skyline, they are silent, they are keeping their ghosts and their thoughts to themselves.

The smoked-glass offices, slung low to the ground, they are still, they are blankly reflecting the haze and shine of the night. Soon, they will resume their business, their coy whispers of ones and zeroes across networks of threaded glass, but now, for a moment, they are hushed. The buses in the depot, waiting for a new day, they are quiet, their metalwork easing and shrinking into place, settling and cooling after eighteen hours of heat and noise, eighteen hours of criss-crossing the city like wool on a loom.

And the clubs in the centre, they are empty, the dancefloors sticky and sore from a night's pounding, the lights still turning and blinking, lost shoes and wallets and keys gathered in heaps.

And the night-fishers strung out along the canal, feeling the sing of their lines in the water, although they are within yards of each other they are saying nothing, watching luminous floats hang in the night like bottled fireflies, waiting for the dip and strike which will bring a centre to their time here, waiting for the quietness and calm they have come here to find.

Even the traffic scattered through these streets: the taxis and the cleaners, the shift-workers and the delivery drivers, even they are held still in this moment, trapped by traffic lights which synchronise red as the system cycles from old day to new, hundreds of feet resting on accelerators, hundreds of pairs of eyes hanging on the lights, all waiting for the amber, all waiting for the green.

The whole city has stopped.

And this is a pause worth savouring, because the world will soon be complicated again.

It's the briefest of pauses, with not time enough to even turn full circle and look at all the lights this city throws out to the sky, and it's a pause which is easily broken. A slamming door, a car alarm, a thin drift of music from half a mile away, and already the city is moving on, already tomorrow is here.

The music is coming from a curryhouse near the football ground, careering out of speakers placed outside to attract extra custom. The restaurant is almost empty, a bhindi masala[1] in one corner, a special korma[1] in the other, and the carpark is deserted except for a young couple standing with their arms around each other's waists. They've not been a couple long, a few days perhaps, or a week, and they are both still excited and nervous with desire and possibility. They've come here to dance, drawn sideways from their route home by the music and by bravado, and now they are hesitating, unsure of how to begin, unfamiliar with the steps, embarrassed.

But they do begin, and as the first smudges of light seep into the sky from the east, from the far side of the city and in towards these streets, they hold their heads high and their backs straight and step together in time to the slide and wheel of the music. They dance with a style more suited to the ball-room than to the Bollywood[2] movies the music comes from, but they dance all the same, hips swinging, waists touching, eyes fixed on eyes. The waiters have come across to the window, they are laughing, they are calling uncle uncle to the man in the kitchen who is finally beginning to clean up after a long night. They dance, and he steps out of the door to watch, wiping his hands on his apron, licking the weary tips of his fingers, pulling at his long beard. They dance, and he smiles and nods and thinks of his wife sleeping at home, and thinks of when they were young and might still have done something like this.

Elsewhere, across the city, the day is beginning with a rush and a shout, the fast whine of office hoovers, the locked slam of lorry doors, the hurried clocking on of the early shifts.

---

[1]**bhindi masala/korma**   dishes often seen on the menu of Indian restaurants
[2]**Bollywood**   the Indian equivalent of Hollywood, based in Mumbai (which was formerly known as Bombay)

But here, as the dawn sneaks up on the last day of summer, and as a man with tired hands watches a young couple dance in the carpark of his restaurant, there are only these: sparkling eyes, smudged lipstick, fading starlight, the crunching of feet on gravel, laughter, and a slow walk home.

Further reading

If you like the way this opening to Jon McGregor's novel mixes a poetic style with a prose account, try reading the opening to Dylan Thomas's play (or is it a poem?) *Under Milk Wood,* which as it opens describes a small Welsh village, its sights, sounds and characters at night.

Activities

The Railway Children

Before you read

1   Visit the ActionAid website www.actionaid.org.uk/ and make brief notes about what the charity's aims are and the sort of work it does.

What's it about?

2   The article begins by focusing on Rohit, a homeless boy living in Bhopal station. With a partner, go through the first five paragraphs and discuss what sort of life he leads, and the problems he faces.

3   The writer gives us quite a lot of factual information about the Bachpan (childhood) project. Re-read what we are told, and then write down a list of at least five key facts about the project. Start:
They deal with children living on the three busiest platforms in Madhya Pradesh.
300 runaways a month . . . (complete, and add five more)

4   Throughout the text, the writer has to convey information often through sentences that carry a good deal of information. For example:

Ashu, 13, who ran away from his violent and alcoholic father in his village in the south of Madhya Pradesh, ended up selling plastic bottles, addicted to solution and beaten up by passengers, police officers and vendors at Katni station.

   a   Can you identify the *main clause* in this sentence (the bit that makes sense on its own) and the *sub-clause* (the bit that has been added in to give more information and is not a complete sentence)?
   b   If you were writing this for a younger readership, how would you turn this into two separate sentences?

Thinking about the text

5   Create a simple fund-raising poster for the Bachpan project and ActionAid. Make sure you include:
   ●   some of the key information from the article
   ●   at least one quote from a railway child
   ●   a persuasive and powerful rhetorical question to draw the reader in (like, 'Do you want children to starve in Africa?').

São Paulo – City of the Future

Before you read

1 When you think about Brazil, what images come into your mind? Draw a spider diagram with 'Brazil' at the centre, and then write any words, phrases or ideas that come to mind around it.

What's it about?

2 The article begins with a helicopter ride, described in the present tense. On your own, go through the text until the moment the helicopter lands, and highlight any verbs that convey the movement and feel of the helicopter ride.

3 Now talk with a partner about the reasons why the writer describes the helicopter ride in the present tense ('the pilot *flicks* the ignition . . .' rather than '*flicked*'). What effect on the reader does this have?

4 From the paragraph beginning 'Avenida Paulista, the city's main drag . . .' note down two phrases that vividly describe the buildings and people as if they were something else (one is a metaphor, the other a simile).

5 The city's mayor, Gilberto Kassab, says that São Paulo's 'inequality is one of the greatest in the world'. With a partner, discuss the descriptions of Guaianases and Paraisopolis. What specific words or phrases support the view of the mayor?

Thinking about the text

6 The writer ends by saying that São Paulo may be becoming, 'against all the odds, a kinder, gentler place'. Look back over the text again and discuss this statement in your group. Do you agree? What evidence is there that things are improving?

7 Write a story called 'Helicopter Landing'. In it, imagine you are a rich businessman or -woman being flown across São Paulo, and having to make an emergency landing in a slum area. You are unhurt, but are lost in the slum. Write the story of what happens to you.

The Missing

Before you read

1   Look at the website for the charity Centrepoint: www.centrepoint. org.uk
    What are its aims, and who is it trying to help?

2   If someone you knew or cared for went missing, how would you go about trying to find them, do you think? Discuss the issue in a group and come up with five recommendations.

What's it about?

3   The extract begins with a sense of vagueness – both from the writer and from 'Dolly' whom we meet in the Strand. How does the writer convey this with his choice of words and the information he gives?

4   Andrew O'Hagan describes Centrepoint as an 'idea of home'. Make a list of the details he describes to support this idea.

5   In the writer's conversation with Racine, we get a good idea of how Racine speaks. How different is the language used from standard non-spoken language? Work with a partner to identify:
    ● added, informal words like 'well', or 'sort of'
    ● changes of tense.

6   O'Hagan also describes Pete McGinlay, one of the people managing the project. Write a short account saying what impression we get of him. Is it a positive one? Support your views with quotations from the text. For example:
    Pete McGinlay seems a kind person, as the writer says he has 'a nice touch' . . .

Thinking about the text

7   What view are we given about the homeless and missing in this text? Discuss in a group:
    ● Is O'Hagan sympathetic to them?
    ● How do you feel about Dolly and Racine? Do you feel sorry for them?
    ● Are there any surprising things you found out about the 'missing'?

8   Write a short script of conversation between Racine and the woman who is looking for her daughter. Remember to include scene directions and a setting for the script, e.g. 'under a street light'.

The Lost Sewer Children

Before you read

1 Do you know where Outer Mongolia is? What image do you have of it as a place? Look at a world map and find out its exact location. What sort of place do you think it is, compared with the UK?

What's it about?

2 The first paragraph presents us with two startling facts. The first is about the weather conditions; the second is about the focus for this article – homeless children. On your own, find those two pieces of information and make a brief note about what might be considered shocking or surprising.

3 More worrying factual information about the homeless children follows in the next paragraph. What do we find out? What more positive information does the article also provide? Create a bullet list of key information.

4 The writer seems to suggest that the crisis of homelessness was caused by a number of things. With a partner, can you find what they are, and then write a short summary of the causes in your own words. Start: The problem of homelessness was caused by . . .

5 This article, although quite objective and factual, also uses some quite strong emotional, visual images to get its point across. On your own, re-read the text, pick out one image and write a sentence describing its effect on the reader.

Thinking about the text

6 In groups, discuss how different the life of a child who has been part of a family of nomadic herders would be compared with that of a child living in the city.

7 Write a short story called 'Escape from the Sewers' in which you write about living as a child in Ulan Bator's sewers and then being helped by a charity such as Save the Children. You may need to re-read the text and do some more research on Ulan Bator.

Little Dorrit

Before you read

1 Discuss in small groups: do you like Sundays? What's good about them – and what is not? Do you find yourself thinking the week-end's almost over and feeling depressed, or thankful you still have one more day to relax?

What's it about?

2 The first paragraph sets the tone for the extract and demonstrates many features common to Dickens's novels:
   • powerful adjectives and verbs to describe sights and sounds
   • use of repeated words or phrases for emphasis
   • long, complicated sentences followed by shorter ones that are almost not sentences at all.

   Work with a partner and find examples of each of these in the paragraph. Then discuss what overall effect and atmosphere are created.

3 Clennam appears in paragraph 2, and we find out about him in the text that follows. Discuss in groups:
   • What are his views about churches and Sundays? (He describes different types of Sunday – can you find each one, e.g. the dreary Sunday of his childhood?)
   • Why does he feel like this?

4 Look at the paragraph beginning 'He crossed by St Paul's'. Make notes on:
   • where Clennam is going
   • what his journey is like
   • the description of the house he arrives at and his attitude to it.

Thinking about the text

5 Compare Dickens's style with that of a modern writer you have read recently. Prepare a short presentation for a small group in which you explain, with examples, how the two styles compare and contrast.

6 Why do you think Clennam is visiting his mother? Write a short script in which you show them meeting. For example:
   Scene: Mrs Clennam's bedchamber. One small candle burning.
   Clennam: *(peering)*   Are you asleep, mother?
   Old Mrs Clennam: No, I am not! Come towards me. I wish to speak to you.

Embankment at Night, Before the War

Before you read

1   Debate the following topic in your class or group:
    'Is it better to give money to a charity than directly to beggars or the homeless?'

What's it about?

2   With a partner, discuss what story the poem tells. What happens in it?
    Start: **The poet, while walking along the Embankment at night . . .**

3   The rain is personified by the use of the words 'furtive' and 'slinks'. Look up these words if you don't know what they mean, and then write a sentence explaining why they fit the poem and the poet's feelings.

4   How does Lawrence use short lines, questions and punctuation to add drama and action to the poem? Make brief notes and then discuss your answers with a partner.

Thinking about the text

5   In a group, re-read the poem and discuss the following questions:
    • How is Lawrence's indecision shown in the poem?
    • Why does he run for his 'life'? What do you think he is frightened of?
    • Why, at the end of the poem, does he say he wants 'to forget'?

6   Write your own poem, based on a similar situation of seeing a homeless person or down-and-out in a specific place, such as by a river, under a bridge etc. Try to get the same sense of drama as Lawrence, by using exclamation marks and short lines.
    You could begin:
    Under the bridge
    In the warm summer's evening as the moon . . .

If Nobody Speaks of Remarkable Things

Before you read

1 As a class, remain completely silent for two minutes. Concentrate on listening to the sounds around you. Then, make notes on sounds:
   - within 50 metres (the next classroom, in the corridor, just outside the window . . .)
   - within 100 metres (the stairs in the school, the car park . . .)
   - beyond that (birds in the sky, roads in the distance . . .).

What's it about?

2 Draw a table like the one below, and list all the nouns, verbs, adjectives and adverbs related to sound from the start of the text to 'and it stops'.

Nouns	Verbs	Adjectives	Adverbs
hum	sings	loudest	quietly

3 The impression of the city is partly conveyed by some vivid similes and metaphors, such as 'loose drains and manhole covers clack-clacking like cast-iron castanets'. Work with a partner to find at least two other similes or metaphors throughout the text.

4 This novel's language has been described as being like poetry. Some of the features of poems are:
   - the use of non-sentences (lines that are not complete on their own)
   - non-standard punctuation (not using capital letters or full stops)
   - use of repetition
   - use of sound and rhythm.
   In groups, go through the text and discuss whether you agree that the text is poetic. Support your views with examples.

Thinking about the text

5 Have you ever lain awake at night for a long time? What sounds could you hear?
   Write a short account of what it was like. (If you haven't, write it from your imagination.)

6 On the surface, there doesn't seem to be much of a story here – but what about characters? Are there any? Could you say the city is a character or not? Make brief notes about your ideas.

Compare and contrast

1   Which of the texts in this section has affected you most? Have you learned something new, found out something surprising, or been shocked or saddened by what you have read? Write about your chosen text or texts, explaining why it or they had such an effect.

2   The text about São Paulo features contrasts between rich and poor. Choose any other text from this section that deals with rich and poor and write a short comparison of them, saying which seems the more positive.

3   *The Railway Children* and *The Lost Sewer Children* both deal with children who are living in terrible conditions. Write a letter from a railway child in India to a child in Ulan Bator in which you describe your experiences and how you feel now you have been reunited with your family.

4   Create a large poster for display, in which you take powerful descriptions based on the sounds, sights and smells of cities from the different texts, writing them onto the sheet, with appropriate pictures or photos around them.

5   Create a short play in a group. It can be based on any of the texts in which a charity is working to help people, like Centrepoint in *The Missing* or ActionAid in *The Railway Children*. Develop a play in which new arrivals are discovered or come to the charity. Where have they come from? What will happen to them?

6   Write your own story called 'Penthouse and Pavement'. It should feature two characters, each with their own section of the text; the first lives in a rich, comfortable penthouse flat, the other on the streets or in a slum. Alternate paragraphs or chapters between the two voices. You can use the first person (I) or the third person (he/she).

4 Gangs, groups, friends and foes

This section is about the different groups and combinations of people in cities, and, in particular:

- their sense of belonging to particular groups and gangs
- the threats they face and how they deal with them
- the extent to which they are outsiders in their communities, and how they themselves deal with those they consider outsiders.

In *The Outsiders*, we learn how the idea of family is much more than Ponyboy's two brothers, whilst in *The Well-dressed Girl Gangs of Paris* we find out how traditional ideas of gangs have changed. *The Kite Runner* and *Tanglewreck* both show us that gangs and allegiances exist both in different cultures and in fictional worlds, whilst *The Whisper* and *Box* offer vivid portraits of gang life on the streets of the UK.

Activities

1 Take a large piece of paper and write the word 'Gang' in the middle. Then, around it, write as many connected ideas and words as you can. Once you have finished, compare what you have written with someone else in your class, and then between you work on a definition of a 'gang'.

2 Talk with a partner about your earliest memory of arguing with another boy or girl of a similar age to you (outside your family). How old were you, and what was the cause of the argument? Was it resolved, and how do you get on with that person now – if you still know them?

3 Several of the characters you will meet in this section have unusual names (Crow, Ponyboy and Sodapop to name a few), some of them given to them by their parents, some they have made up themselves. If you could choose another name – something more

unusual and original than the one you have now (which may be unusual anyway) – what would you choose, and why?

4   Most gangs have leaders. Write a 'job description' for a gang leader in the form of a 'Wanted' advert, starting:

Wanted: gang leader. Must be . . .

Tanglewreck

by Jeanette Winterson

This extract presents a world in which a society lives beneath the streets with its own rules and customs. We see the 'real' world through the eyes of its people – and a very strange view of it they have!

Silver had never seen anything like the underground world of the Throwbacks.

She followed Gabriel down a narrow passage about six inches deep in water. She had no shoes on, and running through the city had torn her socks. Now she was footsore and soaked, but she didn't say anything, just hoisted up her jeans and pyjamas to keep them dry, and walked as quickly as she could. Bits of rubbish were floating about in the water; old crisp packets and burger boxes, and she was glad when they began to move slightly uphill, and the water shallowed out to indented puddles in the clay floor.

Gabriel didn't speak to Silver until they were able to walk side by side.

'This be the way to the Chamber, but we must go by the Devils.'

'Who are the Devils?'

'You shall see them.'

The roof of the passage was getting higher, when suddenly Gabriel doused[1] his torch in a puddle and pulled Silver into an opening in the wall. As they stood still and silent as statues, she could hear voices approaching, and then she saw four men wearing red waterproof suits and full-face helmets with some kind of air filter on the front. They carried high-pressure water guns. She guessed they were for the maintenance of the drains or something like that. Whatever they were, they weren't devils, but Gabriel was trembling.

---

[1]**doused**   put out the light

As soon as the men had gone by, towards the culvert[2] where the Mammoth had come in, Gabriel took Silver's hand and they started on their journey again. He was fearful, and kept looking round.

'It's all right, Gabriel,' said Silver. 'They are human beings like us. Um, well, like me, but men, and grown up. They aren't devils.'

'Did you not see their red bodies and their heads of monsters and their weapons?'

'Those were just waterproof clothes and water guns and some sort of safety helmet, that's all. When they take it off they look like humans, like Updwellers.'

'They cannot take off their heads and bodies,' said Gabriel, 'and I have seen them use their water-weapons. Water is soft but the Devils magic it hard as iron.'

'It's pressurised[3],' said Silver.

---

[2]**culvert**   drain
[3]**pressurised**   emitted under high pressure so that (in this case) water becomes very powerful

'You do not know them,' said Gabriel. 'It is Goliath they seek.'

'The Mammoth.'

'Yea. The Devils will kill him with their weapons.'

'Gabriel,' said Silver, 'do you ever go above ground?'

'We cannot live Upground. We can go there but we cannot live there. We would be killed.'

'Who would kill you?'

'Devils or Wardens or the soldiers, or the White Lead Man.'

Silver couldn't understand this at all, so she fell silent and looked around her to see what these tunnels and passages were.

They were built of brick, and here and there steel ladders were anchored to the walls, leading upwards, she supposed, to the pavement and all those metal plates and grilles[4] that you can see when you walk around the city. She had never thought about what was underneath all those plates and grilles. She had never guessed that there might be a whole world.

A rumbling through the wall made her think that they must be near a Tube[5] train station. She glanced at Gabriel; he didn't seem bothered by the noise.

'What's that?' she said, to see if he knew what it was.

'That be the Long Wagon,' said Gabriel. 'Updwellers use him when they come down here. They fear to walk here by themselves. They come all together in the Long Wagon.'

'Why do they come down here – the Updwellers?'

Silver knew that everybody used the Tube to travel round the city, but she wanted to know what Gabriel thought about it.

'It be their loneliness,' he said. 'Updwellers be lonely for the ground they come from. They come here to remember.'

Silver was beginning to realise that Gabriel's world was not like her own world one bit. But then her world had a lot wrong with it, so she wasn't going to say anything rude about his.

'Updwellers lived here once. Look and see.'

---

[4] **grilles**   open-meshed metal covers
[5] **Tube**   the underground railway system in London

Gabriel opened a little door in the wall and led her on to a deserted platform.

At first it looked like any other Tube station platform, but then Silver realised that the posters on the walls were from the Second World War, because all the people in them were wearing gas masks.

'Updwellers,' repeated Gabriel, and sure enough, they came to a row of rotting stripy mattresses, with blankets still thrown on them, and here and there old newspapers and magazines.

'Air-raid shelters[6],' said Silver, who had read about the war.

'This be the time when all people dwelt underground,' said Gabriel.

Silver didn't believe this was true, but she didn't want to argue, and she was fascinated by this caught moment of Time. It was as though Time had got trapped here and couldn't move on. She didn't feel like she did when she went to a museum and saw lots of old things; she felt as though Time existed differently here. Even though the people had gone away and gone forward, Time itself was left here, or a piece of Time, anyway, as real and solid as the mattresses and tin mugs.

The dirty faded signs on the wall said ALDGATE WEST.

'My work be to find supper,' said Gabriel. 'I may not return without our supper.'

'Where are you going to find that?' asked Silver, wondering why anyone ate supper in the early hours of the morning.

'Here,' said Gabriel, and he disappeared.

Now Silver was alone in the dark, listening to the rats and mice scurrying about their business. She shut her eyes and visualised[7] her little room at Tanglewreck, with the fire lit, and whatever food she had been able to steal from under Mrs Rokabye's selfish and sharp eyes. She supposed that Mrs Rokabye had arranged everything with Abel Darkwater, but did

---

[6]**air-raid shelters**   places where people went to escape the bombing raids during World War II

[7]**visualised**   imagined

that mean she was really bad, or just greedy and stupid? Grown-ups were always worrying about money, she knew that, but what did you need if you could eat and sit in front of the fire and read books? That was what Silver would do with her money.

She wondered if the Throwbacks had any money . . .

Just then Gabriel reappeared, dragging a large sack.

'Pizza,' he said, 'from the Pizza Hut.'

'You've been to Pizza Hut?' asked Silver disbelievingly.

'My mother Eden be from the Kingdom of Italy. There be a Hut up a stretch from this place and at this hour a Short Wagon comes and two Updwellers bring these boxes to the Hut. It be a depot for food. Come.'

Dragging his sack, he hurried along the deserted platform and disappeared into the tunnel where the trains came through. Not wanting to be left behind, Silver ran after him.

Further reading

If you like this sort of story, in which a sympathetic 'underclass' is joined by the main hero or heroine, you might like to read Philip Pullman's *Northern Lights* (Scholastic Point, 1995). There, too, a girl (similar to Silver in *Tanglewreck*) with ownership of a special object, in that case the Golden Compass, finds herself siding with the Gyptians – river dwellers whose children are being kidnapped by a powerful organisation.

Piper

by Meg Harper

In this story, set about 50 years in the future, children are at risk in the city and are under threat from an unnamed disease, which also attacks adults. In this extract, Crow, the young leader of a group of homeless children who live on the edge of the city, is about to return from the city to his secret hideout where the children he has befriended live.

There were appreciative gasps from the girls in the audience as he picked up one of the firestaffs which lay on the floor and lit the wick[1] ends from his makeshift brazier.

Then he started his show. Once alight, the firestaff whizzed from one hand to the other in a dizzying figure of eight. People shuffled backwards, excited but slightly alarmed now. The firestaff circled Crow's neck, dived beneath his legs, flipped under one knee, then the other. Suddenly he was lighting a second staff and the crowd pulled back still further, gasping its admiration and fear. It was impossible to tell which end of the staff was which, where one ended and the other began. Crow was a white-chested, whirling stick-man silhouetted in a nimbus of roaring fire. Money was raining into the hat that he had put out. Crow was grim-faced with concentration but inside he was smiling.

His eyes, his nerves, his muscles were completely focused on the dancing staffs but his ears were still alert for the sound of any threat. He had not survived on the streets of the city without discovering the instincts of the wild animal. He knew what he had heard in the distance. Police sirens. And coming his way. Unlicensed busking[2] was an offence; he'd been warned often enough. And there were no licences for fire. But it drew in the crowds and was as honest a money-spinner as anything else.

---

[1]**wick**   the thread in the centre of a candle or, in this extract, a 'firestaff'
[2]**busking**   performing entertainment on the street

It angered Crow that the police bothered with him. What would they have him do? Drugs? Robbery? Darker deeds that he didn't want to think about? He listened, foxlike, assessing the proximity[3] of the threat. Money was still flying but if the police came any nearer, he would run. Fire was his provider and protector; he couldn't afford to lose it.

Crow darted into the sandstone tunnel and hugged the damp, crumbling wall. He fought to get control of his breathing so that he could listen and check. No, no one was following him. He never took chances though. You didn't hesitate; you just ran. There was no time to waste. All he ever stopped for was to hide his bucket – the one he filled with water from the river in case of accident – which was cumbersome[4] and noisy. The firestaffs he slung across his back and the money went straight in his body belt. He would only stay here in the caves and tunnels which burrowed into the sandy rock that bounded the city's greasy river for long enough to be sure that there was absolutely no threat of pursuit. The police rarely pursued anyone this far. Only kids lived in here; only kids dared to and then only out of desperation. The caves were said to have been inhabited during prehistoric times; the network of tunnels had been dug out during the world war a hundred years ago, for the city people to hide from German bombers. But other stories abounded, rumours to make you quake. So most people avoided them and the police, charged with rounding up street kids but hard-pressed and short-staffed, left well alone. Kids on the streets they occasionally dealt with; to the kids in the sandstone they turned a blind eye.

But Crow wouldn't live there; he had a horror of caves and tunnels for reasons of his own. His squat was the bottom of a long-abandoned mill, a few kilometres upstream, which he guarded fiercely from other squatters with his fire and any

---

[3]**proximity**   nearness
[4]**cumbersome**   clumsy and inconvenient because of its size

missiles he could find. It wasn't ideal. Though overgrown and with no access any more, the steep riverbank that rose above it bounded a Cratz country park. He dreaded being discovered by some interfering rich Cratz walking a dog. He couldn't attack them with fire and wood – if he did the police would want him for more than unlicensed busking. But he'd been all right so far, mostly sleeping in the day. Though he caught fish from the river in the early morning, he never cooked it there, waiting to do that in the city at night. He couldn't risk being given away by the smoke of a fire and the smell of cooking. Only the police seemed to care about the number of kids on the streets of the city; for everyone else they had become part of the landscape, like litter. But in the suburbs and the village enclaves[5] where the Cratz all lived – that was something else. Crow would be as welcome in the country park as a heap of steaming dog turds.

Just as Crow was about to head out of the tunnel to retrieve his bucket – the night was young, it was worth finding another pitch and giving another show – he heard panting and a kid blundered into him.

'Uh!' gasped the kid, winded by the impact. He'd been running hard. 'Who's that?'

Crow didn't think twice but grabbed the boy by the neck, spun him round and locked his arm across his chest. With his free hand, he flicked his lighter to examine his prisoner. The boy's eyes rolled back in his head, trying to see who had captured him.

'Crow?' he squeaked and Crow felt the child relax against him.

Crow shook his head and let the boy loose. He didn't question how the kid knew who he was. He was well-known in the city. 'Stupid,' he said. "You've got to be quieter – and watch where you're going. You won't survive long if you carry on like that.'

'Yes, Crow, sorry, Crow,' said the boy, still breathing hard.

---

[5]**enclaves**　places where groups of people live separately from others who may have a different cultural background

'Don't apologize,' said Crow, harshly. 'It's you, you should say sorry to. You could have got yourself killed. Supposing I'd been someone dangerous? Or supposing I'd thought I was being attacked? Don't you know the risks? Kids in the city – they go missing all the time, and no one even notices. You were very lucky.'

'I know, Crow – but I haven't been here long. It's hard.' There was a sob in the boy's voice that he was fighting to suppress. Crow looked him up and down in the light of his flame, assessing whether he was telling the truth. Yes, the boy still looked soft.

'Parents dead?' Crow asked, more gently.

The boy nodded. 'My mum, anyway,' he said. 'My dad went off ages ago, when she got sick. He was frightened he'd get it, I think.'

'I'm sorry,' said Crow.

'She was ill a long time,' said the boy, his voice breaking. 'I thought she might be one of the ones who got better.'

'You'd best come with me,' said Crow, his voice gruff. 'I can show you a thing or two that'll help.'

The boy hesitated, trying to gulp back his tears.

'You know who I am,' said Crow. 'It's up to you whether you trust me.'

'I'll trust you,' the boy sniffed.

'Good decision,' said Crow. 'What's your name?'

'Timbo.'

'Right, Timbo. Follow me.'

Further reading

Meg Harper's other books are mostly written for younger readers, but if you liked this you might also like *The Ghost in the Gallery* (Lion Publishing, 2001), which deals with a girl who is struggling to talk to her father and ends up communicating with an old portrait painting of someone who shares her name.

The Well-dressed Girl Gangs of Paris

by Adam Sage

This article describes how conventional ideas of gangs have been
challenged by groups of girls living on some Paris estates. How do
they dress, and why do they join gangs?

When police learnt that rival gangs were planning a showdown
in Chelles, east of Paris, they prepared for the sort of violence
that has become routine in France's troubled suburbs.

But even the most hardened officers were stunned as they
arrived at the scene. The participants in what has become
known as the battle of Chelles bus station were all girls aged
between 14 and 17.

'They were fighting like the toughest of boys,' a policewoman who saw the confrontation this month said. 'They had
knives, screwdrivers, sticks and teargas and they were really
going for each other. There must have been about 100 of them –
some taking part and some there as spectators. It was quite
frightening and if we hadn't intervened quickly, it would have
ended in a bloodbath.'

Eight girls were arrested and France was caught in
anguished debate over *les petites terreurs*[1] copying the brutal
behaviour of their male counterparts, a concern that has been
heightened by a 140 per cent increase in female adolescent violence since 2002.

When *The Times* met some of the girls last week, they were
revealed as ordinary adolescents brought up on multi-ethnic
housing estates where violence has become the norm. They
dress with style, use make-up, talk in sweet tones – and think
that teargas and kitchen knives are appropriate for settling a
teenage dispute over boys.

---

[1] *les petites terreurs*   literally, 'the little terrors'; could be interpreted as
'young terrorists'

Awa, for instance, is a member of the girl's gang from Meaux, outside Paris, which confronted rivals from Noisiel, a town 25 miles (40 kilometres) away, at the bus station in Chelles, where they all attend a sixth-form college.

'It all began because one of the Noisiel girls started hanging around the boys in Meaux,' said the 16-year-old, who was wearing a black jacket and pristine white blouse. 'We phoned her up and told her to stop. You don't start going out with our boys if you're from Noisiel. The girl took the call badly and said she was coming down with some of her friends to do us in. So we had to meet them.'

There was an initial clash by the 613 bus stop in Chelles on a Friday afternoon, with a dozen or so girls from each side kicking and punching each other. When that ended without a clear winner, the adolescents sent text messages to arrange another confrontation for the next Monday. This time they brought knives, other weapons and self-defence sprays containing a form of teargas.

'We quite often have to deal with girls' violence these days,' said the policewoman. 'But it's usually four of five of them having a punch-up. I've never seen a pitched battle between gangs of girls like that before, although I'm not completely surprised because they all seem to want to imitate the boys these days. They swear and spit and are really aggressive.'

With turf wars[2] between male gangs a common feature of the French suburbs, which have become synonymous with high immigration, segregation, riots, crime and drugs, it was only a matter of time before the practice spread to girls, she said.

'It's all about defending your territory,' said Jenaba, another 16-year-old participant in the battle of Chelles. 'We grew up together in Meaux, we have been friends since primary school and we go dancing together. It's only natural that we should stick together against the Noisiel gang.'

When asked whether there was an ethnic dimension to the fight, she reacted with surprise. 'It's not the blacks against the Arabs or anything like that. We're all mixed up together. It's just one estate against another.'

'Some of the girls are incredibly violent these days.' Mohammed, a 16-year-old boy, said. 'They're tougher than us. Just the other day a girl in school chased a boy all the way around the grounds with a knife. He had to climb up a tree to get away from her.'

Further reading

Although this is a factual account, there are many stories about girl gangs or groups and the power they wield. On the more humorous side there are films such as *Mean Girls* (2004), but more serious are novels such as *Girl Gang* written by Pete Johnson and illustrated by Lucy Su (Graffix/A & C Black, 2000) and factual studies such as *Odd Girl Out: The Hidden Culture of Aggression in Girls* by Rachel Simmons (Harvest Books, 2003).

---

[2]**turf wars**   bitter struggles for territory, power, control

The Whisper
by Bali Rai

In this extract Billy, the narrator, is on the way home from his girl-friend's house after having fallen asleep. It is three in the morning.

Outside, the night air was fresh and chilly and I clapped my hands together as I walked home, trying to keep out the cold. Falling asleep in my clothes didn't help. I crossed the street and walked past a weary-looking working girl who asked me for a cigarette. I found my pack and offered it to her.

'Thanks,' she said, smiling at me. Two of her front teeth were missing and her hair looked like copper wire. And in her eyes I saw the lack of feeling that my mum's eyes showed whenever she remembered her past.

'No worries,' I replied, putting my fags away. I walked round onto the main road and then turned down the side street that ran parallel to Della's, two minutes from home.

Behind me I heard a screech of tyres and turned to see a black Fiat Punto pull up. Two youths wearing baseball caps got out. I held my position, wary but unafraid. I didn't know who they were and hadn't done anything to upset them so I wasn't worried. As they made to walk into a house, one of them nodded at me, letting me relax a little. They were just local rude boys – new to the area maybe. I nodded back and turned to walk on –

Then the lights went out as a pain like an electric shock sent down your spine hit me with its full force.

Ever since I was a little kid I'd heard stories about people being mugged or beaten up. The local paper carried news about daily street robberies. There were people all over our city who had been caught off guard by the kind of people who had beaten me up and robbed me of my possessions. But it had never happened to me before and as I lay in my bed the following morning, nursing my bruises, I felt ashamed and angry and helpless. I kept playing the mental images over and over in my head, like my own little movie, only in this version things were different: I hadn't ignored the youths. Instead I had realized what they were all about and run – not turned my back like some innocent fool. Or I had faced them down, beaten them up. Alternatives that acted as a defence mechanism against the feelings of embarrassment that welled up inside my chest.

No matter how many times I tried to change the ending in my head though, it didn't alter what had happened. I had woken up lying face down in the street, checked my pockets and found that they'd taken my mobile, my money and my mini-disc player. I had limped home but hadn't woken anyone up, and in the morning my mum had left for work by the time I went downstairs to the kitchen. Nanny, without making too much fuss, helped to clean me up a bit and put antiseptic lotion on my cuts. He sent me back upstairs again and rang work to let them know I wouldn't be coming in. Now he was sitting by my bed with a cup of green tea.

'Yuh know any of dem man from las' night?' he asked me as I took the cup from him.

'Nah – I ain't never seen them before.'

'Dem never say a word?'

I shook my head. 'I thought they was just some local rud-ies, Nanny. You know – some new faces an' that,' I told him.

'An' dem drive a black Fiat?' he continued.

'Yeah – all lowered[1], with alloys[1] and spoilers[1].'

'You see whether dem Asian or black or what?'

I tried to picture them. I could see the caps on their heads and the sportswear but I couldn't really make out the faces.

'I can't remember.'

Nanny put his hand on my shoulder. 'Yuh get some res', my yout'.'

---

[1] **lowered/alloys/spoilers**   the car's suspension had been dropped, the wheel-hubs changed, and parts (spoilers) added to reduce wind resistance and enable more speed

'Don't tell Mum, Nan.'

He gave me a quizzing look. I shrugged before replying.

'I don't want her gettin' stressed. She's got enough wrinkles – she don't need me adding no more. I got mugged. It happens . . .'

'Seen,' replied Nanny. 'But yuh can mek up yuh own story, bwoi. Me never lie to Rita before and me nah go start – '

'Just let me talk to her,' I said, before taking a sip. The tea was strong and bitter but the warmth of it made me feel better.

Not that I'd been too badly injured. I had a swollen lip, a cut under my eye and some bruising around my body. Nothing that I hadn't experienced before from fighting as a kid. The real injury was to my pride. I'd always had this idea in my head that I could walk around the roughest parts of the city and not get done over – because I knew the score. And I'd been wrong. Which hurt more than the bruises and the cuts.

'I'm gone,' said Nanny. 'The dinner nah go cook itself.'

'I'll be down in a bit,' I told him.

'Seen,' he replied, leaving the room and closing the door behind him gently.

Out of habit I reached over to the side table for my mobile but it wasn't there. The two lads had taken it. At first I winced as a pain shot through my side, but then I smiled to myself as I remembered Della losing her own phone a few months earlier. She was one of those people who kept all her numbers in the sim card memory and nowhere else. Like loads of others, she didn't have a clue what her best friends' numbers actually were. They just came up as names on her phone screen so she hadn't bothered to memorize them. Just like me. Luckily, I didn't have to go through all the hassle that Della had to. Maybe because I had too much time on my hands, or perhaps because I was organized, I had downloaded all my numbers onto my computer's hard disk.

I looked over at the dusty laptop and remembered Nanny's mate, Tek Life, getting it for me. He told me that he'd *'emancipate de bloodclaat t'ing'*[2] from a friend in the education department and that's exactly what he had done. Nanny had joked that his name should have been Ronseal. I'd given him a hundred notes for it and the thing worked brilliantly. I got off the bed and went to my desk, left over from my time at school – not that I'd ever used it. I turned the laptop on and waited for the software to load so that I could pull Will's mobile number up. Once I'd written it down on a bit of paper. I headed downstairs again and rang him, hoping that he'd have his mobile on at work.

Further reading

Bali Rai deals with gangs and street life in many of his other novels, such as *The Crew* (Corgi, 2003) in which the characters in *The Whisper*, such as Billy and Della, are first introduced. You might also like *What's Your Problem?* (Barrington Stoke, 2003), which introduces a different character, Jaspal, and his struggle to survive as the only Asian teenager in a village.

---

[2]***emancipate de bloodclaat t'ing***   *set free* (or steal) *the bloody thing* (in Jamaican slang)

The Outsiders
by S. E. Hinton

This extract is from the beginning of a novel written by 17-year-old S. E. Hinton about the gangs in her school, and published in 1967. Here the narrator, Ponyboy, describes his family and friends and explains how he was attacked by rival gang members.

When I stepped out into the bright sunlight from the darkness of the movie house, I had only two things on my mind: Paul Newman[1] and a ride home. I was wishing I looked like Paul Newman – he looks tough and I don't – but I guess my own looks aren't so bad. I have light-brown, almost-red hair and greenish-grey eyes. I wish they were more grey, because I hate most guys that have green eyes, but I have to be content with what I have. My hair is longer than a lot of boys wear theirs, squared off in back and long at the front and sides, but I am a greaser and most of my neighbourhood rarely bothers to get a haircut. Besides, I look better with long hair.

I had a long walk home and no company, but I usually lone it anyway, for no reason except that I like to watch movies undisturbed so I can get into them and live them with the actors. When I see a movie with someone, it's kind of uncomfortable, like having someone read your book over your shoulder. I'm different that way, I mean, my second-oldest brother, Soda, who is sixteen-going-on-seventeen, never cracks a book at all, and my oldest brother, Darrel, who we call Darry, works too long and hard to be interested in a story or drawing a picture, so I'm not like them. And nobody in our gang digs movies and books the way I do. For a while there, I thought I was the only person in the world that did. So I loned it.

---

[1]**Paul Newman**   an American film star, especially popular in the 1960s and 1970s

Soda tries to understand, at least, which is more than Darry does. But then, Soda is different from anybody; he understands everything, almost. Like he's never hollering[2] at me all the time the way Darry is or treating me as if I was six instead of fourteen. I love Soda more than I've ever loved anyone, even Mom and Dad. He's always happy-go-lucky and grinning, while Darry's hard and firm and rarely grins at all. But then, Darry's gone through a lot in his twenty years, grown up too fast. Sodapop'll never grow up at all. I don't know which way's the best. I'll find out one of these days.

Anyway, I went on walking home, thinking about the movie, and then suddenly wishing I had some company. Greasers can't walk alone too much or they'll get jumped, or someone will come by and scream 'Greaser!' at them, which doesn't make you feel too hot, if you know what I mean. We get

---

[2]**hollering**   shouting

jumped by the Socs. I'm not sure how you spell it, but it's the abbreviation for the Socials, the jet set. the West-side rich kids. It's like the term 'greaser,' which is used to class all us boys on the East Side.

We're poorer than the Socs and the middle class. I reckon we're wilder, too. Not like the Socs, who jump greasers and wreck houses and throw beer blasts for kicks, and get editorials in the paper for being a public disgrace one day and an asset to society the next. Greasers are almost like hoods; we steal things and drive old souped-up cars and hold up gas stations and have a gang fight once in a while. I don't mean I do things like that. Darry would kill me if I got into trouble with the police. Since Mom and Dad were killed in an auto wreck, the three of us get to stay together only as long as we behave. So Soda and I stay out of trouble as much as we can, and we're careful not to get caught when we can't. I only mean that most greasers do things like that, just like we wear our hair long and dress in blue jeans and T-shirts, or leave our shirt-tails out and wear leather jackets and tennis shoes or boots. I'm not saying that either Socs or greasers are better; that's just the way things are.

I could have waited to go to the movies until Darry or Sodapop got off work. They would have gone with me, or driven me there, or walked along, although Soda just can't sit still long enough to enjoy a movie and they bore Darry to death. Darry thinks his life is enough without inspecting other people's. Or I could have got one of the gang to come along, one of the four boys Darry and Soda and I have grown up with and consider family. We're almost as close as brothers; when you grow up in a tight-knit neighbourhood like ours you get to know each other real well. If I had thought about it, I could have called Darry and he would have come by on his way home and picked me up, or Two-Bit Mathews – one of our gang – would have come to get me in his car if I had asked him, but sometimes I just don't use my head. It drives my brother Darry nuts when I do stuff like that, 'cause I'm supposed to be smart;

I make good grades and have a high IQ and everything, but I don't use my head. Besides, I like walking.

I about decided I didn't like it so much, though, when I spotted that red Corvair trailing me. I was almost two blocks from home then, so I started walking a little faster. I had never been jumped, but I had seen Johnny after four Socs got hold of him, and it wasn't pretty. Johnny was scared of his own shadow after that. Johnny was sixteen then.

I knew it wasn't any use though – the fast walking. I mean – even before the Corvair pulled up beside me and five Socs got out. I got pretty scared – I'm kind of small for fourteen even though I have a good build and those guys were bigger than me. I automatically hitched my thumbs in my jeans and slouched, wondering if I could get away if I made a break for it. I remembered Johnny – his face all cut up and bruised, and I remembered how he had cried when we found him, half-conscious, in the corner lot. Johnny had it awful rough at home – it took a lot to make him cry.

I was sweating something fierce, although I was cold. I could feel my palms getting clammy and the perspiration running down my back. I get like that when I'm real scared. I glanced around for a pop bottle or a stick or something – Steve Randle, Soda's best buddy, had once held off four guys with a busted pop bottle – but there was nothing. So I stood there like a bump on a log while they surrounded me. I don't use my head. They walked around slowly, silently, smiling.

'Hey, grease,' one said in an over-friendly voice. 'We're gonna do you a favour, greaser. We're gonna cut all that long greasy hair off.'

He had on a madras[3] shirt. I can still see it. Blue madras. One of them laughed, then cursed me out in a low voice. I couldn't think of anything to say. There just isn't a whole lot you can say while waiting to get mugged, so I kept my mouth shut.

---

[3]**madras**   soft cotton with a plaid-type design, originally made in Madras (now Chennai) in India

'Need a haircut, greaser?' The medium-sized blond pulled a knife out of his back pocket and flipped the blade open.

I finally thought of something to say. 'No.' I was backing up, away from that knife. Of course I backed right into one of them. They had me down in a second. They had my arms and legs pinned down and one of them was sitting on my chest with his knees on my elbows, and if you don't think that hurts, you're crazy. I could smell English Leather shaving lotion and stale tobacco, and I wondered foolishly if I would suffocate before they did anything. I was scared so bad I was wishing I would. I fought to get loose and almost did for a second; then they tightened up on me and the one on my chest slugged me a couple of times. So I lay still, swearing at them between gasps. A blade was held against my throat.

'How'd you like that haircut to begin just below the chin?'

It occurred to me then that they could kill me. I went wild. I started screaming for Soda, Darry, anyone. Someone put his hand over my mouth, and I bit it as hard as I could, tasting the blood running through my teeth. I heard a muttered curse and got slugged again, and they were stuffing a handkerchief in my mouth. One of them kept saying, 'Shut him up, for Pete's sake, shut him up!'

Then there were shouts and the pounding of feet, and the Socs jumped up and left me lying there, gasping. I lay there and wondered what in the world was happening – people were jumping over me and running by me and I was too dazed to figure it out. Then someone had me under the armpits and was hauling me to my feet. It was Darry.

'Are you all right, Ponyboy?'

He was shaking me and I wished he'd stop. I was dizzy enough anyway. I could tell it was Darry though – partly because of the voice and partly because Darry's always rough with me without meaning to be.

'I'm okay, Quit shaking me, Darry, I'm okay.'

He stopped instantly. 'I'm sorry.'

He wasn't really. Darry isn't ever sorry for anything he does. It seems funny to me that he should look just exactly like my father and act exactly the opposite from him. My father was only forty when he died and he looked twenty-five and a lot of people thought Darry and Dad were brothers instead of father and son. But they only looked alike – my father was never rough with anyone without meaning to be.

Darry is six-feet-two, and broad-shouldered and muscular. He has dark-brown hair that kicks out in front and a slight cowlick[4] in the back – just like Dad's – but Darry's eyes are his own. He's got eyes that are like two pieces of pale bluegreen ice. They've got a determined set to them, like the rest of him. He looks older than twenty – tough, cool, and smart. He would be real handsome if his eyes weren't so cold. He doesn't understand anything that is not plain hard fact. But he uses his head.

I sat down again, rubbing my cheek where I'd been slugged the most.

Darry jammed his fists in his pockets. They didn't hurt you too bad, did they?'

They did. I was smarting and aching and my chest was sore and I was so nervous my hands were shaking and I wanted to start bawling, but you just don't say that to Darry.

'I'm okay.'

Sodapop came loping[5] back. By then I had figured that all the noise I had heard was the gang coming to rescue me. He dropped down beside me, examining my head.

'You got cut up a little, huh, Ponyboy?'

I only looked at him blankly. 'I did?'

He pulled out a handkerchief, wet the end of it with his tongue, and pressed it gently against the side of my head. 'You're bleedin' like a stuck pig.'

'I am?'

---

[4]**cowlick**   a curl of hair that has been plastered into place with grease or water
[5]**loping**   walking with long strides

'Look!' He showed me the handkerchief, reddened as if by magic. 'Did they pull a blade on you?'

I remembered the voice: 'Need a haircut, greaser?' The blade must have slipped while he was trying to shut me up. 'Yeah.'

Soda is handsomer than anyone else I know. Not like Darry – Soda's movie-star kind of handsome, the kind that people stop on the street to watch go by. He's not as tall as Darry, and he's a little slimmer, but he has a finely drawn, sensitive face that somehow manages to be reckless and thoughtful at the same time. He's got dark-gold hair that he combs back – long and silky and straight – and in the summer the sun bleaches it to a shining wheat-gold. His eyes are dark brown – lively, dancing, recklessly laughing eyes that can be gentle and sympathetic one moment and blazing with anger the next. He has Dad's eyes, but Soda is one of a kind. He can get drunk in a drag race[6] or dancing without ever getting near alcohol. In our neighbour-hood it's rare to find a kid who doesn't drink once in a while. But Soda never touches a drop – he doesn't need to. He gets drunk on just plain living. And he understands everybody.

He looked at me more closely. I looked away hurriedly, because, if you want to know the truth, I was starting to bawl. I knew I was as white as I felt and I was shaking like a leaf.

Soda just put his hand on my shoulder. 'Easy, Ponyboy. They ain't gonna hurt you no more.'

'I know,' I said, but the ground began to blur and I felt hot tears running down my cheeks. I brushed them away impatiently. 'I'm just a little spooked, that's all.' I drew a quivering breath and quit crying. You just don't cry in front of Darry. Not unless you're hurt like Johnny had been that day we found him in the vacant lot. Compared to Johnny I wasn't hurt at all.

Soda rubbed my hair. 'You're an okay kid, Pony.'

I had to grin at him – Soda can make you grin no matter what. I guess it's because he's always grinning so much himself. 'You're crazy, Soda, out of your mind.'

---

[6]**drag race** car race in which fast acceleration over a short distance is key

Darry looked as if he'd like to knock our heads together. 'You're both nuts.'

Soda merely cocked one eyebrow, a trick he'd picked up from Two-Bit. 'It seems to run in this family.'

Darry stared at him for a second then cracked a grin. Sodapop isn't afraid of him like everyone else and enjoys teasing him. I'd just as soon tease a full-grown grizzly[7]; but for some reason, Darry seems to like being teased by Soda.

Our gang had chased the Socs to their car and heaved rocks at them. They came running towards us now – four lean, hard guys. They were all as tough as nails and looked it. I had grown up with them, and they accepted me, even though I was younger, because I was Darry and Soda's kid brother and I kept my mouth shut good.

Steve Randle was seventeen, tall and lean, with thick greasy hair he kept combed in complicated swirls. He was cocky, smart, and Soda's best buddy since grade school. Steve's specialty was cars. He could lift a hubcap quicker and more quietly than anyone in the neighbourhood, but he also knew cars upside-down and backward, and he could drive anything on wheels. He and Soda worked at the same gas station – Steve part time and Soda full time – and their station got more customers than any other in town. Whether that was because Steve was so good with cars or because Soda attracted girls like honey draws flies, I couldn't tell you. I liked Steve only because he was Soda's best friend. He didn't like me – he thought I was a tagalong and a kid; Soda always took me with them when they went places if they weren't taking girls, and that bugged[8] Steve. It wasn't my fault; Soda always asked me, I didn't ask him. Soda doesn't think I'm a kid.

Two-Bit Mathews was the oldest of the gang and the wisecracker[9] of the bunch. He was about six feet tall, stocky in build,

---

[7]**grizzly**   a type of bear notorious for its aggressive behaviour
[8]**bugged**   annoyed
[9]**wisecracker**   joker

and very proud of his long rusty-coloured sideburns. He had grey eyes and a wide grin, and he couldn't stop making funny remarks to save his life. You couldn't shut up that guy; he always had to get his two-bits worth in. Hence his name. Even his teachers forgot his real name was Keith, and we hardly remembered he had one. Life was one big joke to Two-Bit. He was famous for shoplifting and his black-handled switchblade[10] (which he couldn't have acquired without his first talent), and he was always smarting off to the cops. He really couldn't help it. Everything he said was so irresistibly funny that he just had to let the police in on it to brighten up their dull lives. (That's the way he explained it to me.) He liked fights, blondes, and for some unfathomable reason, school. He was still a Junior at eighteen and a half and he never learned anything. He just went for kicks. I liked him real well because he kept us laughing at ourselves as well as at other things. He reminded me of Will Rogers – maybe it was the grin.

If I had to pick the real character of the gang. It would be Dallas Winston – Dally. I used to like to draw his picture when he was in a dangerous mood, for then I could get his personality down in a few lines. He had an elfish face, with high cheekbones and a pointed chin, small, sharp animal teeth, and ears like a lynx. His hair was almost white it was so blond, and he didn't like haircuts, or hair oil either, so it fell over his forehead in wisps and kicked out in the back in tufts and curled behind his ears and along the nape of his neck. His eyes were blue, blazing ice, cold with a hatred of the whole world. Dally had spent three years on the wild side of New York and had been arrested at the age of ten. He was tougher than the rest of us – tougher, colder, meaner. The shade of difference that separates a greaser from a hood wasn't present in Dally. He was as wild as the boys in the down-town outfits, like Tim Shepard's gang.

In New York, Dally blew off steam in gang fights, but here, organized gangs are rarities – there are just small bunches of

---

[10]**switchblade**   flick-knife

friends who stick together, and the warfare is between the social classes. A rumble,[11] when it's called, is usually born of a grudge fight, and the opponents just happen to bring their friends along. Oh, there are a few named gangs around, like the River Kings and the Tiber Street Tigers, but here in the Southwest there's no gang rivalry. So Dally, even though he could get into a good fight sometimes, had no specific thing to hate. No rival gang. Only Socs. And you can't win against them no matter how hard you try, because they've got all the breaks and even whipping them isn't going to change that fact. Maybe that was why Dallas was so bitter.

He had quite a reputation. They have a file on him down at the police station. He had been arrested, he got drunk, he rode in rodeos,[12] lied, cheated, stole rolled drunks, jumped small kids – he did everything. I didn't like him, but he was smart and you had to respect him.

Johnny Cade was last and least. If you can picture a little dark puppy that has been kicked too many times and is lost in a crowd of strangers, you'll have Johnny. He was the youngest, next to me, smaller than the rest, with a slight build. He had big black eyes in a dark tanned face; his hair was jet-black and heavily greased and combed to the side, but it was so long that it fell in shaggy bangs across his forehead. He had a nervous, suspicious look in his eyes, and that beating he got from the Socs didn't help matters. He was the gang's pet, everyone's kid brother. His father was always beating him up, and his mother ignored him, except when she was hacked off at something, and then you could hear her yelling at him clear down at our house, I think he hated that worse than getting whipped. He would have run away a million times if we hadn't been there. If it hadn't been for the gang, Johnny would never have known what love and affection are.

I wiped my eyes hurriedly. 'Didya catch 'em?'

---

[11]**rumble**   a fight between street gangs
[12]**rodeos**   exhibitions of horse-riding skills as entertainment

'Nup. They got away this time, the dirty . . .' Two-Bit went on cheerfully, calling the Socs every name he could think of or make up.

'The kid's okay?'

'I'm okay.' I tried to think of something to say. I'm usually pretty quiet around people, even the gang. I changed the subject. 'I didn't know you were out of the cooler, yet, Dally.'

'Good behaviour, Got off early.' Dallas lit a cigarette and handed it to Johnny. Everyone sat down to have a smoke and relax. A smoke always lessens the tension. I had quit trembling and my colour was back. The cigarette was calming me down. Two-Bit cocked an eyebrow. 'Nice-lookin' bruise you got there, kid.'

I touched my cheek gingerly. 'Really?'

Two-Bit nodded sagely. 'Nice cut, too. Makes you look tough.'

Tough and *tuff* are two different words. *Tough* is the same as rough; *tuff* means cool, sharp – like a tuff-looking Mustang or a tuff record. In our neighbourhood both are compliments.

Steve flicked his ashes at me. 'What were you doin', walkin' by your lonesome?' Leave it to good old Steve to bring up something like that.

'I was comin' home from the movies. I didn't think . . .'

'You don't ever think,' Darry broke in, 'not at home or anywhere when it counts. You must think at school, with all those good grades you bring home, and you've always got your nose in a book, but do you ever use your head for common sense? No sirree, bub. And if you did have to go by yourself, you should have carried a blade.'

I just stared at the hole in the toe of my tennis shoe. Me and Darry just didn't dig each other. I never could please him. He would have hollered at me for carrying a blade if I *had* carried one. If I brought home Bs, he wanted As, and if I got As, he wanted to make sure they stayed As. If I was playing football, I should be in studying, and if I was reading, I should be out playing football. He never hollered at Sodapop – not even when

Soda dropped out of school or got tickets for speeding. He just hollered at me.

Further reading

If you like *The Outsiders* you might like to read other books by S. E. Hinton, such as *Rumble Fish* (Collins, 1992) and *That was Then, This is Now* (Collins, 1992) which also deal with gang culture and friendships in smaller towns in the USA. Both *The Outsiders* and *Rumble Fish* were turned into films by Francis Ford Coppola, best known as director of *The Godfather* trilogy. Another book which features a strong central teenage character who feels he is a misfit and doesn't initially belong is *Catcher in the Rye* by J. D. Salinger (1951).

Box   161

Box

by Mark Powell

> This extract from the beginning of the novel introduces us to Pow-Wow, one of the main characters, and then to the gang to which he belongs.

It hasn't been a good year in north-west London (NWL). It has all been too much. Too many gangstas killing gangstas; too many mural memorials being painted on walls; too many scores being settled; too many girls giving birth; too many vials of contaminated rock. And there has been no sign of the sun and summer is already here.

Pow-Wow stands by his bedroom window, toking on a stick[1] and watching the Jubilee line rattle past. Watching the red and silver pipe slide into the station that looks old with rusty bricks. Watching the sour faces peer from the Metropolitan trains that run the fast track.

Pow-Wow likes Tuesdays. He likes their brightness even though the morning sky outside is still a shroud.[2]

Pow-Wow knows what his house looks like from the rails – bitty, loose-tiled, sloping sideways – but he is not afraid to look passengers in the eyes as they stare up at his bare black torso.

Tyrone! Brenda, his mum shouts.

I know! Pow-Wow (real name Tyrone) shouts back, without taking his gaze off the trains.

He scrunches the joint into an ashtray and reaches for his crash helmet that lies on the floor.

Topless, he leaves the room and locks his door. Jumps down the stairs two at a time and pushes past a younger brother who stands in the hallway yapping on a mobile. Pow-Wow grabs the

---

[1] **toking on a stick**   smoking cannabis
[2] **shroud**   covering, usually of a dead person

phone and cancels the call while slipping it into his trouser pocket.

– I've told you before, young blood, he says to the brother.

Outside, mopeds fill the street.

Pow-Wow high-fives a few of the nearest riders before mounting his own bike and popping the engine.

Twice a week the All-Star Chapter Pack patrols the neighbourhood for outsiders.

The Pack is for the 15–17 age group; their penultimate[3] posting before hoping to hit the big league with the Daddy-Boy Homing Crew, who command the postcode.[4]

Most of the All-Stars have worked their way up through the junior battalions and under-15 squads to find themselves taking orders from Mister B, All-Star Number One.

The scooters, the moped, the bikes, the peds, the rockets are the badge of belonging. Those who ride pillion[5] dream of the day of ownership. Some under-15s steal the wheels to ride illegally. The police have little interest in the kids.

The tattoos smudged onto dark skin identify the loyalties. All-Star written in Japanese characters and/or a star covering the edge of the shoulder.

Despite the dull weather, most of the Pack go half-naked and slouch on scooters with loose jeans falling over hips as they pull back throttle and thrash along terraced streets. The roads are pot-holed and dotted with broken drain-covers. The riders swerve and bounce their way round the patrol. Cars swing into the kerb to avoid the convoy.

The peds slow down as they pass a basketball court in which a dozen youth run about in singlets and high boots. The faces on the playground are scrutinized. All locals.

---

[3]**penultimate**   the one before the last
[4]**command the postcode**   rule or control the area
[5]**ride pillion**   are passengers

Box   163

A black Mercedes sounds its horn and Mister B throws his arm up to halt the patrol. He spins his scooter around the back of the car and brakes by the driver's door.

– Wha's happening, Papa? Mister B asks, offering a hand.

They shake with three components: a standard grip, a thumb grip, ended with a grasp around the wrist.

– Mister B, my mantra, Papa replies through sunglasses.

– Keeping it tight, yeah?

– Damn right.

There is a stiff pause; Papa checks his mirror, Mister B checks over shoulder at the crew.

– How's business? Mister B asks.

– Nice. Real nice. Sugar and spice. We'll need some carriers later in the week.

– We're always ready, you know it.

– I know it. Things are expanding at such a rate, man. This town is booming.

Mister B smiles; he knows it will not be too long before he is enjoying some of the high life. Has been All-Star Number One for a year now. A promotion to the Daddies is due.

Papa reaches into the passenger seat's headrest. A heavy gold chain slips down the forearm.

– Slip that into the pants, Papa says, pulling out a wad of notes along with a plastic bag of weed.

Mister B stuffs the package into his trousers.

– You're running things good. You know we look out for you, Papa adds.

– That ain't no lie.

– We know you can show it.

Mister B offers an appreciating smile in reply.

The electric window purrs up and the face of Papa is gone. The Mercedes moves off the kerb and away.

Mister B's mobile rings. A lookout has spotted a stranger on Neasden Lane. The crew take off.

Neasden Lane is dusty from the works site next to the station. It is smokey from the lorries trundling in and out of the yard.

The Pack arrives at the scene to find an unknown kid strutting up the hill. They slam brakes and leap off seats to make a grab. Mister B takes the throat and pushes the boy against an advertising hoarding.

– Where you heading, brother? Mister B spits.

– I ain't done nothing, man, the kid gurgles back, trying to move his neck out of the grip.

– How old are you?

– Ten, replies the kid.

Mister B stares into the nervous face. Notices the bubbles of sweat on his eyebrows.

– Where do you live, boy?

– Wembley Cent.

– Why are you walking the hill?

– To the subway, head uptown.

– You know where you are?

– Yeah, man. I'm down seeing a blood.

– Who's your man?

– Menalic Jackson.

Mister B checks his crew's faces for recognition.

One of the riders gives a slight rock of the head.

– This is All-Star patch. You know that?

– No.

– You're young, dude. You don't want to start making foes.

– No, no, I hear you.

Mister B puts his hand into his trousers and takes the knife.

The kid's face panics.

– No, man, this ain't right, he pleads.

– You seen a blade before? Mister B says, flipping the weapon from hand to hand.

– I'm easy, man.

– Oh yeah? Mister B says, suddenly pressing it against the kid's head.

The kid waves his hands in front of his face and grunts.

The watching pack snigger.

Box   165

Mister B lowers the knife and grins.

– So you don't want to get plunged. Cool. So strip.

– Say what?

– I said strip.

Slowly the kid undresses, folding his trousers and T-shirt, left standing in knickers.

– And the shreddies.

The kid pulls in air from one side of his mouth, making a sucking sound, pulls down the red underwear.

A dozen motors wait in the corner of the Sports Centre car park. Fifty faces avoid each other and scour the surroundings for the arrival of Pow-Wow.

Ileasha stands next to Pimp Papa, who drops his arm over her shoulder and whispers words that make her laugh and make her easy. And Papa is tempted to skim his hand down her curves but he will wait. No one looks at the two of them as they tease but focus on the weed sticks being passed about.

Track suits, baggy jeans, topless torsos, basketball tops and shorts, high socks with sneakers. Individuals strutting around in circles. Some shadow-boxing and kick-boxing moves going on in jest. The anticipation of violence pushing aggression into the veins of the spectators.

The young All-Stars show off in front of the adults, who sit on BMW bonnets and nod heads to the beats pumping from drop-top sound systems.

Ego staring at the concrete. Swinging his arms in circles to keep muscles warm. Flopping his head from side to side to encourage flexibility. Popping his eyes up occasionally to catch the glimpse of a friend with a wink and then slipping back into his trance.

Pow-Wow limps slowly across the open space from the road. Arriving alone now that Ileasha is angry and Mister B is neutral.

Pow-Wow strips off his top as he gets near. Throws it to an All-Star.

Ego, already topless, steps into the middle and pulls his head back so far onto his neck that he is peering down the nose.

A few seconds of staring, standing within inches of each other, copied from the pro fighters. Pow-Wow a small boy compared to the bulk and maturity of Ego. Two-stone difference in weight, with half a foot discrepancy in height.

They both throw their arms up into right angles.

Ego edges forward, Pow-Wow edges back.

Pow-Wow moves in, Ego moves out.

And then they both attack at the same time and meet in a flash of fists.

Pow-Wow throws punch after punch, trying to break through the size of his opponent.

Ego offers less in the way of quantity but aims a single big shot for every two of Pow-Wow's.

Pow-Wow's shots make the sound of a slap. Ego's thud.

They back off, take stock of the situation, then charge back into the slugging.

The crowd loses its passion. Fisticuffs are not as much fun as they remember.

Ego lands a heavy one and Pow-Wow folds. He bends over and tries to catch hold to recover, but Ego is slick and stands back and throws uppercuts to the head and rabbit punches to the kidneys.

Pow-Wow falls and Ego jumps on top, pressing his knees onto his opponent's arms. With Pow-Wow's head exposed, Ego starts dropping bombs.

Moving his face from side to side, Pow-Wow tries to escape the torrent of blows.

Pimp Papa steps in and hurls the new All-Star Number One off the battered Pow-Wow.

The crowd disperse quickly. The Daddies have business and pleasure to attend to. The All-Stars have new hierarchies[6] to plot.

---

[6]**new hierarchies**   changed ranking of status; changes in the pecking order

Box   167

From the floor, Pow-Wow notices Ileasha drop a kiss on the cheek of Pimp Papa. Pow-Wow knows Papa's game. And he watches Pimp turn to Ileasha and give her elbow the slightest stroke before he sinks into a car.

Mister B tries to offer consolation but Pow-Wow can read the lack of interest in his eyes. Mister B is already gone; he's with the future. While Pow-Wow is left pummelled on a car park facing a reduced role in the Pack. Facing a lengthy wait before he can consider reaching Mister B's position. Facing humiliation in front of friends and Ileasha.

Ileasha waits near to where Pimp Papa departed. She looks over at the bruised Pow-Wow. She looks so much older for her age – much older than Pow-Wow. And her girlfriends call her over. And she goes. Without a word.

Further reading

Mark Powell's novel *Snap* (Phoenix, 2001) is perhaps even more 'gritty' than *Box* and takes its characters out of London as they flee from a crime which they might be blamed for. Once again, it is about allegiances – who is with you, who is against you. You might also like to read *Caught in the Crossfire* (Orion, 2003) and *The Edge* (Orion, 2002) by Alan Gibbons which both feature teenagers faced with difficult personal decisions about groups, friends or family.

The Kite Runner

by Khaled Hosseini

> The following extract describes an encounter between a bullying older boy, and the narrator and his childhood friend Hassan. It explores the older boy's behaviour and character, and how the narrator and his friend face up to the danger he presents.

They weren't shooting ducks after all. As it turned out, they hadn't shot much of anything that night of July 17, 1973. Kabul awoke the next morning to find that the monarchy[1] was a thing of the past. The king, Zahir Shah, was away in Italy. In his absence, his cousin Daoud Khan had ended the king's forty-year reign with a bloodless coup.[2]

I remember Hassan and I crouching that next morning outside my father's study, as Baba[3] and Rahim Khan sipped black tea and listened to breaking news of the coup on Radio Kabul.

'Amir agha?' Hassan whispered.

'What?'

'What's a "republic"?'

I shrugged. 'I don't know.' On Baba's radio, they were saying that word, 'republic', over and over again.

'Amir agha?'

'What?'

'Does "republic" mean Father and I will have to move away?'

'I don't think so,' I whispered back.

Hassan considered this. 'Amir agha?'

'What?'

'I don't want them to send me and Father away.'

---

[1] **monarchy**   system of government headed by a king or queen
[2] **bloodless coup**   a takeover of government that does not involve any deaths by fighting
[3] **Baba**   respectful term for father

I smiled. '*Bas*, you donkey. No one's sending you away.'

'Amir agha?'

'What?'

'Do you want to go climb our tree?'

My smile broadened. That was another thing about Hassan. He always knew when to say the right thing – the news on the radio was getting pretty boring. Hassan went to his shack to get ready and I ran upstairs to grab a book. Then I went to the kitchen, stuffed my pockets with handfuls of pine nuts, and ran outside to find Hassan waiting for me. We burst through the front gates and headed for the hill.

We crossed the residential street and were trekking through a barren patch of rough land that led to the hill when, suddenly, a rock struck Hassan in the back. We whirled around and my heart dropped. Assef and two of his friends, Wali and Kamal, were approaching us.

Assef was the son of one of my father's friends, Mahmood, an airline pilot. His family lived a few streets south of our home, in a posh, high-walled compound[4] with palm trees. If you were a kid living in the Wazir Akbar Khan section of Kabul, you knew about Assef and his famous stainless-steel brass knuckles, hopefully not through personal experience. Born to a German mother and Afghan father, the blond, blue-eyed Assef towered over the other kids. His well-earned reputation for savagery preceded him on the streets. Flanked by his obeying friends, he walked the neighborhood like a Khan[5] strolling through his land with his eager-to-please entourage.[6] His word was law, and if you needed a little legal education, then those brass knuckles were just the right teaching tool. I saw him use those knuckles once on a kid from the Karteh-Char district. I will never forget how Assef's blue eyes glinted with a light not entirely sane and how he grinned, how he *grinned*, as he pummeled that poor kid unconscious. Some of the boys in Wazir Akbar Khan had nick-named him Assef *Goshkhor*, or Assef 'the Ear Eater'. Of course, none of them dared utter it to his face unless they wished to suffer the same fate as the poor kid who had unwittingly inspired that nickname when he had fought Assef over a kite and ended up fishing his right ear from a muddy gutter. Years later, I learned an English word for the creature that Assef was, a word for which a good Farsi[7] equivalent does not exist: 'sociopath'.

Of all the neighborhood boys who tortured Ali, Assef was by far the most relentless. He was, in fact, the originator of the Babalu jeer, *Hey, Babalu, who did you eat today? Huh? Come on, Babalu, give us a smile!* And on days when he felt particularly inspired, he spiced up his badgering a little, *Hey, you flat-nosed Babalu, who did you eat today? Tell us, you slant-eyed donkey!*

---

[4]**compound**   style of house in some countries; the building and a central
   yard are enclosed by a high wall, and usually house an extended family
[5]**Khan**   an eastern nobleman, chief
[6]**entourage**   following
[7]**Farsi**   Afghan language

Now he was walking toward us, hands on his hips, his sneakers kicking up little puffs of dust.

'Good morning, *kunis*!' Assef exclaimed, waving. 'Fag,' that was another of his favorite insults. Hassan retreated behind me as the three older boys closed in. They stood before us, three tall boys dressed in jeans and T-shirts. Towering over us all, Assef crossed his thick arms on his chest, a savage sort of grin on his lips. Not for the first time, it occurred to me that Assef might not be entirely sane. It also occurred to me how lucky I was to have Baba as my father, the sole reason, I believe, Assef had mostly refrained from harassing me too much.

He tipped his chin to Hassan. 'Hey, Flat-Nose,' he said. 'How is Babalu?'

Hassan said nothing and crept another step behind me.

'Have you heard the news, boys?' Assef said, his grin never faltering. 'The king is gone. Good riddance. Long live the president! My father knows Daoud Khan, did you know that, Amir?'

'So does my father,' I said. In reality, I had no idea if that was true or not.

'"So does my father,"' Assef mimicked me in a whining voice. Kamal and Wali cackled in unison. I wished Baba were there.

'Well, Daoud Khan dined at our house last year.' Assef went on. 'How do you like that, Amir?'

I wondered if anyone would hear us scream in this remote patch of land. Baba's house was a good kilometer away. I wished we'd stayed at the house.

'Do you know what I will tell Daoud Khan the next time he comes to our house for dinner?' Assef said. 'I'm going to have a little chat with him, man to man, *mard* to *mard*. Tell him what I told my mother. About Hitler. Now, there was a leader. A great leader. A man with vision. I'll tell Daoud Khan to remember that if they had let Hitler finish what he had started, the world would be a better place now.'

'Baba says Hitler was crazy, that he ordered a lot of innocent people killed,' I heard myself say before I could clamp a hand on my mouth.

Assef snickered. 'He sounds like my mother, and she's German; she should know better. But then they want you to believe that, don't they? They don't want you to know the truth.'

I didn't know who 'they' were, or what truth they were hiding, and I didn't want to find out. I wished I hadn't said anything. I wished again I'd look up and see Baba coming up the hill.

'But you have to read books they don't give out in school,' Assef said. 'I have. And my eyes have been opened. Now I have a vision, and I'm going to share it with our new president. Do you know what it is?'

I shook my head. He'd tell me anyway; Assef always answered his own questions.

His blue eyes flicked to Hassan. 'Afghanistan is the land of Pashtuns. It always has been, always will be. We are the true Afghans, the pure Afghans, not this Flat-Nose here. His people pollute our homeland, our *watan*. They dirty our blood.' He made a sweeping, grandiose gesture with his hands. 'Afghanistan for Pashtuns, I say. That's my vision.'

Assef shifted his gaze to me again. He looked like someone coming out of a good dream. 'Too late for Hitler,' he said. 'But not for us.'

He reached for something from the back pocket of his jeans. 'I'll ask the president to do what the king didn't have the *quwat* to do. To rid Afghanistan of all the dirty, *kasseef* Hazaras.'

'Just let us go, Assef,' I said, hating the way my voice trembled. 'We're not bothering you.'

'Oh, you're bothering me,' Assef said. And I saw with a sinking heart what he had fished out of his pocket. Of course. His stainless-steel brass knuckles sparkled in the sun. 'You're bothering me very much. In fact, you bother me more than this Hazara[8] here. How can you talk to him, play with him, let

---

[8]**Hazara**   a minority group/tribe in Afghanistan

him touch you?' he said, his voice dripping with disgust. Wali and Kamal nodded and grunted in agreement. Assef narrowed his eyes. Shook his head. When he spoke again, he sounded as baffled as he looked. 'How can you call him your "friend"?'

But he's not my friend! I almost blurted. *He's my servant*! Had I really thought that? Of course I hadn't. I hadn't. I treated Hassan well, just like a friend, better even, more like a brother. But if so, then why, when Baba's friends came to visit with their kids, didn't I ever include Hassan in our games? Why did I play with Hassan only when no one else was around?

Assef slipped on the brass knuckles. Gave me an icy look. 'You're part of the problem, Amir. If idiots like you and your father didn't take these people in, we'd be rid of them by now. They'd all just go rot in Hazarajat where they belong. You're a disgrace to Afghanistan.'

I looked in his crazy eyes and saw that he meant it. He *really* meant to hurt me. Assef raised his fist and came for me.

There was a flurry of rapid movement behind me. Out of the corner of my eye, I saw Hassan bend down and stand up quickly. Assef's eyes flicked to something behind me and widened with surprise. I saw that same look of astonishment on Kamal and Wali's faces as they too saw what had happened behind me.

I turned and came face to face with Hassan's slingshot. Hassan had pulled the wide elastic band all the way back. In the cup was a rock the size of a walnut. Hassan held the slingshot pointed directly at Assef's face. His hand trembled with the strain of the pulled elastic band and beads of sweat had erupted on his brow.

'Please leave us alone, Agha,' Hassan said in a flat tone. He'd referred to Assef as 'Agha,' and I wondered briefly what it must be like to live with such an ingrained sense of one's place in a hierarchy.

Assef gritted his teeth. 'Put it down, you motherless Hazara.'

'Please leave us be, Agha,' Hassan said.

Assef smiled. 'Maybe you didn't notice, but there are three of us and two of you.'

Hassan shrugged. To an outsider, he didn't look scared. But Hassan's face was my earliest memory and I knew all of its subtle nuances, knew each and every twitch and flicker that ever rippled across it. And I saw that he was scared. He was scared plenty.

'You are right, Agha. But perhaps you didn't notice that I'm the one holding the slingshot. If you make a move, they'll have to change your nickname from Assef "the Ear Eater" to "One-Eyed Assef", because I have this rock pointed at your left eye.' He said this so flatly than even I had to strain to hear the fear that I knew hid under that calm voice.

Assef's mouth twitched. Wali and Kamal watched this exchange with something akin to fascination. Someone had challenged their god. Humiliated him. And, worst of all, that someone was a skinny Hazara. Assef looked from the rock to Hassan. He searched Hassan's face intently. What he found in it must have convinced him of the seriousness of Hassan's intentions, because he lowered his fist.

'You should know something about me, Hazara,' Assef said gravely. 'I'm a very patient person. This doesn't end today, believe me.' He turned to me. 'This isn't the end for you either, Amir. Someday, I'll make you face me one on one.' Assef retreated a step. His disciples followed.

'Your Hazara made a big mistake today, Amir,' he said. They then turned around, walked away. I watched them walk down the hill and disappear behind a wall.

Hassan was trying to tuck the slingshot in his waist with a pair of trembling hands. His mouth curled up into something that was supposed to be a reassuring smile. It took him five tries to tie the string of his trousers. Neither one of us said much of anything as we walked home in trepidation, certain that Assef and his friends would ambush us every time we turned a corner. They didn't and that should have comforted us a little. But it didn't. Not at all.

Further reading

The Kite Runner was made into a successful and powerful film in 2007 (directed by Marc Forster) and if, having seen it or read the novel, you are interested in the history of Afghanistan and its effect on ordinary people's lives, you might like to read *A Thousand Splendid Suns*, Hosseini's next novel, published in 2007, which features a greater focus on girls' and women's experiences, or *The Bookseller of Kabul* by Asne Seierstad (Little, Brown, 2003).

Activities

Tanglewreck

Before you read

1   What sorts of places can be found underground? In a group, list all the possible locations, creatures, things and people that can be found underground at any time (e.g. sewers, cellars, rats).

What's it about?

2   Early in the text, it becomes clear that the story is set in the present day, more or less. What evidence can you find to support this? Write a sentence or two to explain your view.

3   The difference between Gabriel and Silver is shown in a number of ways. With a partner, discuss:
   • how they speak differently
   • Gabriel's view of the 'Updwellers' (who are they?).

Thinking about the text

4   Silver says she gets a different idea of time when she compares the old underground station with what museums are like. Discuss in a group:
   • Have you ever visited a place where they have tried to show what a room or a building was like in the past, or seen costumed actors showing how people used to live? How much of a feeling did this give you for the period?
   • Is Silver fair to say that museums don't give you a proper idea of time/history?

5   Many fantasy stories are about societies living in specific places, like the 'Updwellers'. Note down made-up names for people living:
   • by a river, e.g. 'Water-livers'
   • on the sides of a mountain
   • amongst the clouds
   • in marshes or swamps.

   Write the opening 150–200 words of a story about these characters.

Piper

Before you read

1 How do you think society will have changed 50 years from now, especially for children? Will there still be homeless children and runaways, or will society have solved the problem?

What's it about?

2 The extract begins with a vivid portrait of Crow. Working with a partner, jot down answers to these questions:
   a How is Crow earning money?
   b At two points in the opening extract, Crow is described as if he were an animal. Can you find these references? What do they suggest about Crow (and the adults/police)?

3 We learn quite a lot about the society of the town and the city. Some of this is told to us directly, in other cases it is implied. In groups, discuss what we learn about:
   ● the way society views the children Crow looks after
   ● the people referred to as Cratz
   ● the police.

4 How does the author use dialogue to convey Crow's and Timbo's feelings and characters? Make notes about:
   ● Crow's rhetorical questions
   ● words and phrases describing *how* something is said.

Thinking about the text

5 What impression do you get of Crow from this account? From the list below, choose two words that accurately describe him and then justify your decisions to the rest of your group or class:

   gentle   *aggressive*   *athletic*   *weak*   *frightened*
   powerful   *alone*   *slow*   *thoughtful*   *quick-witted*

6 Write an alternative version to the extract, in which Crow is caught by the police and taken back to headquarters to be interrogated. Write it as a story, and describe what happens – is Crow punished, does he escape, or does something else happen?

The Well-dressed Girl Gangs of Paris

Before you read

1   In a group, discuss what the factors are that encourage young people to join groups. Which of the following do you think has the most influence?
   ● Location (school, estate, road)
   ● Family (brother or sister already a member?)
   ● Threats from gang members
   ● Protection

What's it about?

2   The title of this report is designed to draw the reader in. What is interesting or surprising about it?

3   What do we find out about the girls in the gangs? Create and complete a table like the one below.

Where they live/come from:
How they dress/look:
Who is in their gang:
What caused the battle between the gangs:

4   This report contains a number of features you would expect to see in similar articles. Working with a partner, go through the text and identify the following features:
   ● the main incident or news story being reported
   ● information about who was involved, when it happened, why it happened, and where it happened
   ● facts and figures to support the wider story about girl gangs
   ● expert comment
   ● comments from witnesses.

Thinking about the text

5   Imagine you are the boy mentioned in the last paragraph. Write a diary entry for your day at school when the girl appeared and chased you. What happened, and why did it happen?

The Whisper

Before you read

1   Do you know anyone who has been mugged? What happened and what was stolen – if anything? What do people feel like after it has happened – does it make them change their behaviour, or do they carry on as before?

What's it about?

2   Does the beginning of the extract glamorise life on the streets? Look at the description of the woman Billy gives a cigarette to, and write a sentence or two in response to this question.

3   How is the idea of gangs and territory apparent even before Billy is knocked out? With a partner, find any evidence for this, and jot down some notes.

4   The characters of Nanny and Billy are partly conveyed by the use of non-standard spelling or grammar to show how they speak. Copy and complete the table below, adding non-standard forms to the left column and their standard forms to the right.

Non-standard	Standard
Yuh	You
dem	
las'	
I ain't never seen them before	

Thinking about the text

5   The narrator wishes he had acted differently to avoid being mugged. Write a different version of events in which he realises what might happen, and tries to run off. Start:
    They were just local rude boys, but something made me suspicious, so I stopped for a moment . . .

6   In a group, come up with '10 tips to avoid being mugged' for local teenagers. Each tip should start with an imperative verb, such as '*Keep* your mobile out of sight'.

The Outsiders

Before you read

1   Write short descriptions of at least one member of your family and one friend. Try to sum up how they behave, how they look, their characters, and your relationship with them.

What's it about?

2   In groups, list the characters Ponyboy tells us about. Then, on your own, select one and write his name in the centre of a sheet of paper. Based on what Ponyboy tells us, create a spider diagram with key words, quotes and descriptions in note form. For example:

Ponyboy's older brother

Darrel

Works very hard

3   The story is set in the USA in the mid-1960s. Working with a partner, look at the section from 'Anyway, I went on walking home . . .' to 'Need a haircut, greaser?' and find any examples of American vocabulary for which we use different words in the UK (e.g. 'movie-house'/'cinema').

4   There are a variety of images Ponyboy uses to describe his friends and family: 'Soda attracted girls like honey draws flies.' Find at least two more similes or metaphors like this, and write a sentence on each, saying how effective it is.

Thinking about the text

5   Imagine you have the chance to talk to one of the characters in the story. In your group explain why you would choose him, and what questions you would ask about his life.

6   What impression of gangs is given by this extract? Does it glamorise them or attack them? Write a short essay explaining your ideas.

7   Turn the incident when Ponyboy is attacked and then rescued into a short script. Make sure all scene directions and movements are set out correctly. For example:
Boy 1: (*smiling*)   Hey, greaser . . .
Ponyboy looks around for something to defend himself with . . .

Box

Before you read

1   Research the statistics on gang-related crime in the UK for this year. You could select a city or town, and see what you can find out. Are the media right to say that things are getting worse, or do the statistics show something else?

2   Look at a website such as www.headliners.org and then look at the 'stories' section. What do young people have to say about gangs and gang violence? What solutions do they suggest?

What's it about?

3   The opening paragraph sets the scene for the novel. With a partner, discuss:
   * where the story is taking place
   * what problems and issues are facing the area (and how the author uses repetition to make his point)
   * how the last sentence adds to the feeling of gloom.

4   The writer tells us about the 'All-Star Chapter Pack', and uses a lot of vocabulary which suggests an organisation, rather like an army, ready to face or look out for the enemy. Go through the section from 'Twice a week . . .' to 'The Mercedes moves off the kerb and away' and note down and words or phrases that show this.

5   Go through the text and re-read what is said about Mister B. Write a short character study of him, using adjectives supported by evidence from the text. End by saying whether you, as a reader, like or dislike him.

Thinking about the text

6   With a partner, discuss Mark Powell's style. Why does he choose to write dialogue without speech marks? Why does he describe what happens in the present tense rather than the past tense?

7   As a class, debate the following statement:
   'This sort of story should not be read in school because it deals with gang violence, gang language and drug taking.'

The Kite Runner

Before you read

1   Think of the different villains you know from stories you have read or films you have seen. Who sticks out in your mind? How do they behave?

What's it about?

2   Summarise the incident in this extract in a series of simple sentences, for example:

Hassan and the narrator set out to climb the tree.

They are stopped by . . .

3   Work in a group. Divide the group into two and each take either the character of Assef or Hassan. Go through the text and make notes on:

● their appearance
● how they behave
● what sort of person they are.

Then share your ideas within the group or class.

4   How does the writer convey the suspense and tension of the encounter between Hassan and Assef? On your own, copy and complete the table below:

Feature	Example/Quotation
The narrator's comments about how Hassan is really feeling	
Use of action and stillness	
Assef's reactions to Hassan	

Thinking about the text

5   On the surface, Hassan and the narrator are close friends – but what evidence is there that not everything is as it seems?

6   Write a version of the story from the point of view of Hassan. Make sure you don't include the narrator's thoughts. Try to include vivid descriptive details as well as Hassan's feelings and emotions.

Compare and contrast

1   Write a comparison of the three texts – *The Outsiders*, *Box* and *The Kite Runner* – which show confrontations between different people. Comment on:
- what happens
- the people involved
- the location/situation
- where our sympathies lie.

2   Looking at this section as a whole, come up with an alternative title for it. Once you have done so, present your idea to a group, justifying your choice.

3   Write a short essay in which you compare and contrast Crow (from *Piper*) and Gabriel (from *Tanglewreck*). In what ways are they similar and different? Comment in particular on their role as outsiders, and how they view others who do not live in their world.

4   Using the structure of *The Well-dressed Girl Gangs of Paris* as a model, create a news report about a group in which different members take on different roles, for example a reporter, witness, teenagers involved etc. Once you have rehearsed it, perform it in front of the class.

5   Imagine you are a distant cousin of one of the characters in *The Whisper* or *Box,* and have been sent from a quiet village or town to stay with one of the characters. Write an email to a brother or sister, explaining what life is like and your view on the gang world.

6   Choose one of the texts in this section and turn it into a poem. You will need to:
- select powerful lines, words and phrases from the original text
- organise them into a verse format (e.g. two verses of six rhyming lines)
- get rid of unnecessary or irrelevant words.

Then redraft and revise, adding your own words and ideas.
Evaluate your finished poem by comparing it with the original text. Which do you prefer and why?

5 Hear me speak

Sometimes, when we live reasonably comfortable lives ourselves, it can be difficult to understand the challenges other people face, especially in cities which might appear thriving and problem-free to outsiders. In this section you will hear about people in cities whose voices are often not heard, who perhaps feel they are ignored, or get the worst deal and face the worst problems. The extracts range from the young man harassed by police as he goes to work, through to a refugee from a brutal war trying to make his way in a UK school, and to a former gang member in the USA who is providing a platform for those whose voices are not usually heard on radio.

The extracts in this section look at:

- the causes of unrest and resentment from various people and groups
- the opportunities open to marginalised people – or the lack of them
- the role of education in helping people out of poverty and crime
- how people's backgrounds and the environment they grew up in affect their future lives.

Activities

1 Can you recall a time when your voice and your opinions weren't heard or listened to? How did you feel – and what did you do about it? Imagine this was the case all the time: that you felt permanently ignored, permanently as if you were a second-class citizen. What emotions would go through you, and how might you act?

2 Think about television, radio and films. Are there particular people or groups whose voices we don't hear very often? Discuss in a group who these people are and *why* they might not be given their say.

3   *The Big Issue* is a good example of a magazine that gives a voice to people, such as the homeless, who don't usually have a chance to have their say. In particular, there is a section that features poems by homeless people. Imagine you were asked by *The Big Issue* to come up with new ideas for giving homeless people a chance to voice their opinions. List three ideas for articles to add to *The Big Issue* and write down why you think these ideas would work.

4   Imagine there was a collection of poems or stories written by people who have been ignored by society – the poor, the homeless, the old, certain ethnic minorities etc. Design a cover for the book – also called (like this section) *Hear Me Speak*. It must include the title, some sort of picture, drawing or photo, and a short sub-heading, to explain the theme of the book.

Once you have completed it, display your cover designs around the classroom.

Harassment

by Frederick Williams

> This poem's subject is clear from its title, but it also tells a story –
> almost like an anecdote – and it will help if you are clear about the
> difference between accent (how words are pronounced: 'wok' for
> 'work') and dialect (the vocabulary and grammar of a place or
> group of people: 'fe se' / 'for see', instead of 'to see') as you try to
> follow it.

One evening, me a com from wok,
An a run fe ketch de bus,
Two police start fe run me dung,
Jus fe show how me no hav no luck,
Dem ketch me and start to mek a fus
Sas, a long time dem a watch how me
A heng, heng round de shop

Me say me? What? Heng round shop?
From morning me daa wok,
Me only jus stop,
An if onoo tink a lie me a tell,
Gwaan go ask de Manager.

Dem insisted I was a potential thief,
And teck me to de station,
Anyway, dem sen and call me relations,
Wen dem com it was a big relief,
Fe se som one me own colour,
At least, who would talk and laugh wid me,

An me still lock up in a Jail,
So till me people dem insist that
Dem go a me wok to get som proof,
The police man dem nearly hit the roof,

Because dem feel dem was so sure,
That is me dem did have dem eyes on
Boy, I don't know what's rong
With these babylon men,[1]
But dem can't tell one black man,
From de other one,

Anyway, when we reach me wok place,
Straight away de manager recognise me face,
And we go check me card,
Fe se sa me dis clock out
So me gather strength and say to de coppers
Leggo me, onoo don't know wey onoo on about,

---

[1]**babylon men**   men from an oppressive, tyrannical society (Ancient
   Babylon was a very powerful Persian city)

You want fe se dem face sa dem a apologise,
But wen me look pon how me nearly face disgrace,
It mek me want fe kus and fight,

But wey de need, in a babylon sight,
If yu right you rong,
And wen you rong you double rong,

So me a beg onoo, teck heed
Always have a good alibi,
Because even though yu innocent
Someone always a try
Fe mek yu bid freedom goodbye.

Further reading

If you like poetry written in West Indian or Caribbean dialect, then try reading poetry by James Berry or Grace Nichols, or look at collections such as *The Heinemann Book of Caribbean Poetry* (Heinemann, 1992) or *A Caribbean Dozen* (Walker Books, 2007). For a hard-hitting novel that focuses on rap, try Benjamin Zephaniah's *Gangsta Rap* (Bloomsbury, 2004).

Little Soldier

by Bernard Ashley

> Kaninda, the main character in this extract from Bernard Ashley's play, is a refugee from an African country in which two tribal groups have fought a brutal civil war. Kaninda has seen atrocities committed on his family and friends by the Yusulu people, and has now seen another boy, from the Yusulu, at his London school, and deep feelings of hatred and revenge have surfaced.

Act Two
Scene 1

Kaninda's bedroom. Kaninda is sitting looking at an atlas, tracing across a page with a finger. At a knock, he closes the atlas, puts it under a pillow and goes to the door. Laura is there.

LAURA   Kaninda . . .

KANINDA   Yes?

LAURA   Just wondered. Do you want to come out? With me? Don't know what you're doing, but do you want to go for a walk?

Kaninda stares at her: what is this?

It's just, I don't know you, you don't know me. We're in the same house but we're not brother and sister. We're in next door rooms and we're a world apart. Thought we'd try to get to know each other, just for an hour. How about down   10 by the river, where you like to be?

KANINDA   The river?

LAURA   If you like. You like rivers . . .

KANINDA   The River Lasai, I fish, swim with my father . . .

LAURA	But definitely not in this one. No swimming here!
KANINDA	An' no father . . .
LAURA	We've got a few ships. Did you have ships?
KANINDA	(*turning away*) Boats. Boats, just.
LAURA	There's that one at Tate and Lyle's – the sugar ship.

20

KANINDA	Sugar?

Kaninda comes out of his room, shuts his door, and they start walking into the next scene.

Scene 2

The Thames Barrier riverfront, further along than before. We can see the outline of the Thames Barrier. Continuous. Laura and Kaninda walk in from the previous scene. Baz Rosso is sitting on the seat of a swing, his legs out.

KANINDA	This sugar ship. It stays how long?
LAURA	About a week, a big one like that.
KANINDA	To Mozambique.
LAURA	Wherever.

She looks round for Theo and sees Baz Rosso.

BAZ ROSSO	(*over at the ship*) She goes out on the Saturday night tide.
LAURA	Kaninda, this is Baz Rosso.

But Kaninda goes on past Baz Rosso to the wall where he stares across at the ship.

BAZ ROSSO	It's good things I'm hearin' about you, Ken.

30

Theo appears from a shadow.

THEO	Only the best, man, only the best.

Kaninda turns round at this ambush, looks over the wall at the drop, back at the others, takes a defensive stance, clearly deciding which way he'll go if there's trouble.

BAZ ROSSO　Theo tells me, like, you're some mondo fighter.[1] Uh? You got a tongue, have you?

Slowly, defiantly, Kaninda shows his tongue to them all.

Same colour as mine.

THEO　Ken, this guy can help you. He's the main man. What you want? Mobiles, iPods – he can get all that, can't you, Baz?

LAURA　Theo!

KANINDA　Or N'gensi? Yusulu boy, can you get me?

BAZ ROSSO　N'gensi? Who the hell's that?　　40

THEO　African kid. Protected in school like he's some prince.

KANINDA　*(to Theo)* You get me.

THEO　Pos-it-ive! You jus' do the run, Ken, it's the rules, initiation[2], an' then Crew brothers help Crew brothers.

LAURA　I don't believe this!

KANINDA　Then you get N'gensi?

Afterthought.

See if he does this initiation?

---

[1] **mondo fighter**　fictional character featured in the fighting game series *Battle Arena Toshinden*.

[2] **initiation**　a group often requires some trial of strength or courage before an individual is accepted into the group

| THEO | Yeah, I can do anythink. Whenever. The more 50 the better in the Crew. How's about this time tomorrow? After school? |

KANINDA   (*nodding*) Okay.

THEO   But only when you're in the Crew, man.

Kaninda looks back along the wall at the run he's got to do.

KANINDA   So I do this run? What is it?

THEO   See this straight bit of river wall, down to the kids' playground? You run it fast, along the top, which ain't wide, which anyone could walk, slow – but to get in the Crew you run along it like Olympics, an' you do it in under 60 twenny seconds . . .

Kaninda looks along the wall and shrugs.

Or you don't. You're too slow, or you fall off. Which ain't serious this side of the wall, but that . . .

KANINDA   You are wet. I been in rivers . . .

THEO   No, son, you are dead. See, you got to do it at low tide, when all you got twenny foot down is concrete slabs an' old shopping trolleys.

KANINDA   Twenty seconds? No problem!

LAURA   Kaninda! That's suicide!   70

THEO   Top dog!

KANINDA   Then you get Yusulu boy here for the same?

THEO   (*walking Kaninda back along the wall, heading offstage*) Pos-it-ive!

Kaninda kicks off his shoes and starts taking deep breaths. Sergeant Matu appears in his spot.

SERGEANT MATU Pump up! Pump up! You got me? Oxygen! Two full lungs of it! Rope bridges, trees across water, keep your eyes ahead on where you're goin' an' trust your feet. Pump up! I'm telling you. Oxygen for speed and fast blood for clear eyes.

Sergeant Matu disappears.

KANINDA (*looks over the river wall*) Long way down! 80

THEO You reckon N'gensi could do this an' all?

Kaninda shrugs and walks off by the wall.

(*to Baz Rosso*) Got your stop watch?

BAZ ROSSO Don't need no stop watch, I can count.

THEO (*shouts off to Kaninda*) That's it, man!

Start there!

LAURA He can fall! He can kill himself!

THEO   Lor, girl, I done it! I'm Crew!

LAURA   But you're stupid! This is stupid. Initiation!

THEO   Yeah, jus' like christenin'!

He calls to Kaninda, who is offstage.

You ready, Ken. Be hot, man!   *90*

LAURA   Really stupid!

Laura covers her eyes as Baz Rosso raises his hand.

BAZ ROSSO   (*calls*) You ready?

THEO   (*calls*) Do the business, Ken!

LAURA   (*calls*) Be careful!

BAZ ROSSO   (*calls, sweeping down his arm*) Then, go! Avanti!³

THEO   (*calls*) Go, man!

LAURA   (*calls*) Watch out!

She screams at a stumble.

THEO   (*calls*) You're all right, that's it, son. Keep
straight. You're doin' good!

To Baz.

Watch, he's quick! Half way!   *100*

Calls.

Go on, man.

To Laura.

Look at that balance!

LAURA   Look at that idiot!

THEO   Go on! Go on!

Kaninda runs into view.

---

³**Avanti!**   Go! (in Italian)

BAZ ROSSO	Fifteen . . .
LAURA	You've done it! Stop now, stop!
THEO	Great, Ken! You're sool, you!
KANINDA	Yusulu?

He is suddenly thrown off guard, looks around for Faustin N'gensi, and loses his footing.

BAZ ROSSO	Eighteen . . .
LAURA	Kaninda!

110

She rushes forward and grabs at him.

THEO	Ken!

Kaninda falls off the wall on the river side, but he is saved by Laura's hands that have grabbed his arm.

LAURA	Help! Help me!

Theo and Baz Rosso help her to haul him over to safety.

THEO	Pos-it-ive, Laura! You was quick!
BAZ ROSSO	Twenty! Vincitore![4] You made it, boy!
THEO	Great! You're in, Ken, you're in the Crew! See?
KANINDA	(*looking round urgently*) Where's Yusulu?
	You said Yusulu.
THEO	I said you're sool, you – which you are, man. Real sool!
BAZ ROSSO	So, tomorrow we talk tactics and strategy. Uh? I'll see you. Ciao![5]

120

He goes.

---

[4]**Vincitore!**   Victory! (in Italian)
[5]**Ciao!**   Italian for 'Bye!'

THEO	Ciao, man!

LAURA	Ye Gods, Kaninda!

Kaninda bows to Laura and formally shakes her hand.

KANINDA	I thank you. For that.

LAURA	That's all right. Take a life, save a life.

But Kaninda isn't listening to her.

KANINDA	(*to Theo*) Here. Tomorrow. Now you get him? Yusulu.

THEO	Sure, 'cos you're in. We're brothers.

He puts an arm round Theo's shoulder.

C'mon. I'll nick you a Coke off Mal.

He walks Kaninda off, but over his shoulder he says to Laura . . .

Cheers, Lor. Cheers for fixin' it.   130

Kaninda looks round at Laura as he's led off, wiping his mouth with the back of his hand, like smudging lipstick.

KANINDA	Laura?

Further reading

You may like to read the novel upon which the play was based, *Little Soldier* (1991), or read more about the experiences of real child soldiers in Africa or elsewhere, for example in *A Long Way Gone: Memoirs of a child soldier* by Ishmael Beah (2007). You could also visit the website of Human Rights Watch and look at the section on Children's Rights: go to www.hrw.org, click on 'Topics,' then on 'Children's Rights' (left-hand panel) and then on 'Child Soldiers' (right-hand panel) to http://hrw.org/en/topic/children039s-rights/child-soldiers

Ex-gang Member Opens LA Airwaves to Street Voices

by Andrew Glazer

This article explains how a radio DJ in Los Angeles runs a show that allows people suffering from gang violence or pressure to phone in and talk about their lives and problems. We also get an insight into the DJ's own past life and also the place of such a show on commercial radio.

Los Angeles – Curtis confides in a quavering voice that he's been feeling sad and lonely as one of the only college students living in a violent housing project. He's dialed up Bo Taylor, a streetwise radio host who uses his show to converse with and counsel gang members, their worried mothers and others cowering in the dark corners of this sprawling city. Awake and alone in their homes, cars or prison cells, listeners like Curtis are using the former gang member's program on R&B station V100-FM to sound off about increasing street violence, poverty and friction with police.

'I love God, but I'm where I hate life right now,' says Curtis, who does not give his last name.

Taylor, 41, who served time in a juvenile hall,[1] says he understands.

'People will always knock you for being you. Knock you for doing good,' Taylor says. 'You're the first one to come out of projects and go to college, the first one to come out of your family and make something out of yourself. You've got it bad, man . . . Nobody wants you to be successful.'

Taylor doesn't try to offer advice. In the early Sunday morning hours when his show airs, he says, it can be enough for distraught callers to know they aren't alone. With a sandpaper voice, a criminal past and a tendency to leave thick

---

[1] **juvenile hall**   young offenders institution

chunks of dead air during the midnight to 2 a.m. show, Taylor is unlike most others on mainstream commercial radio. And the audience he's after and the subjects he addresses typically are anathema[2] in a dense media market scrapping for ad dollars with market-tested playlists and golden-throated disc jockeys.

It took three years for Taylor and his producer, an established figure in black talk radio who refused to allow his name to be used for this story, to persuade the station to give Taylor a forum. The show has been on the air for a little more than a month, and station officials say they are pleased so far. The Bo Taylor Show debuted[3] as heightened violence between Hispanic[4] and black street gangs ignited fears that violence would spread across the city. Outside the studio, Taylor works to develop truces between rival gangs. He was instrumental in brokering[5] a truce between the Crips and Bloods more than a decade ago.

Taylor refuses to disclose details of his own previous gang ties, fearful that doing so would somehow glorify his criminal past. The father of four instead regularly offers anecdotes about his current activism and self-reform.

'The only way we can all be peaceful in the city is if we all come together and realize the only way we can all be free, the only way we can all be peaceful in the city, is find some common ground,' Taylor told listeners at the start of one show.

On the air one night, he offered condolences to community activist Cynthia Mendenhall. One of her sons was killed in a drive-by shooting last summer; the other shot and killed himself in December as police chased him for driving erratically.

---

[2]**anathema**   object of abhorrence; deeply unpopular
[3]**debuted**   opened with its first show
[4]**Hispanic**   referring to people from the Caribbean islands that were colonised by the Spanish, e.g. Cuba, Puerto Rico
[5]**brokering**   acting as a go-between for different groups

'I don't know what it would be like to lose both your sons and keep soldiering on,' Taylor said. 'I don't know if you're up and listening, but I hope the word is getting to you.'

Another show followed an announcement of a new city-wide anti-gang initiative that calls for making a list of the city's most dangerous gangs. The bald, tattooed host opened up the lines to gang members who lambasted[6] the plan as bad policy. They warned that gangs left off the list would feel affronted and try to raise their profile with stepped-up violence.

'It's like listening in on a conversation that none of us would normally hear,' said civil rights attorney Connie Rice, a guest that night. 'You're not going to only hear from gang interventionists. You are going to hear from shot-callers in gangs calling from prisons.'

Someone who identifies himself as 'Bow Wow' calls from the Jordan Downs projects, the domain of the infamous Grape Street Crips, who appeared on the city's list. Bow Wow says fighting gangs with an increased police presence will heighten community alienation and resentment.

'These kids need to be occupied with field trips, jobs,' he says.

Taylor cuts off 'Bow Wow' and announces a celebrity caller: it turns out 'Lethal Weapon' star Danny Glover has been listening in.

'It's people like you that give me inspiration and help me know that I'm not alone,' Taylor tells him.

The actor/activist returns the compliment.

'It's vice versa as well, Bo,' Glover says. 'You and brothers trying to keep peace in the neighborhood, as a friend of mine says, are trying to tame a lion with a switch. You know that gives me inspiration.'

---

[6]**lambasted**   reprimanded, attacked with words

Further reading

Gang violence in the inner cities of the USA has long been a subject of film-makers, television writers and novelists. Most recently, the acclaimed television series *The Wire* dealt with the lives of poor black families and gangs in Baltimore, and earlier films such as *Boyz n the Hood* (directed by John Singleton, 1991) explored the influence of gangs and parents on the directions chosen by young people. The book *Street Wars: Gangs and the future of violence* by Tom Hayden (The New Press, 2006) explores why gangs exist and some of the solutions needed.

Why Paris is Burning

by Amir Taheri

This article deals with the complex and troubled background to the street riots that occurred in Paris and other areas of France in 2005. France was in a state of emergency, and many people questioned what sort of society existed in the country which could allow such things to happen.

November 4, 2005 – As the night falls, the 'troubles' start – and the pattern is always the same.

Bands of youths in balaclavas[1] start by setting fire to parked cars, break shop windows with baseball bats, wreck public telephones and ransack cinemas, libraries and schools. When the police arrive on the scene, the rioters attack them with stones, knives and baseball bats. The police respond by firing tear-gas grenades and, on occasions, blank shots in the air. Sometimes the youths fire back – with real bullets. These scenes are not from the West Bank[2] but from 20 French cities, mostly close to Paris, that have been plunged into a European version of the *intifada*[3] that at the time of writing appears beyond control.

The troubles first began in Clichy-sous-Bois, an underprivileged suburb east of Paris, a week ago. France's bombastic interior minister, Nicholas Sarkozy, responded by sending over 400 heavily armed policemen to 'impose the laws of the republic', and promised to crush 'the louts and hooligans' within the day. Within a few days, however, it had dawned on anyone who wanted to know that this was no 'outburst by criminal elements' that could be handled with a mixture of braggadocio[4]

---

[1]**balaclavas**   woollen hats which cover most of the face except the eyes
[2]**West Bank**   a section of the Palestine/Israel border where there is frequently conflict
[3]*intifada*   an uprising by Palestinian Arabs in protest against Israeli occupation of the Gaza Strip and West Bank
[4]**braggadocio**   bragging; mock bravery

and batons. By Monday, everyone in Paris was speaking of 'an unprecedented crisis'. Both Sarkozy and his boss, Prime Minister Dominique de Villepin, had to cancel foreign trips to deal with the riots.

How did it all start? The accepted account is that sometime last week, a group of young boys in Clichy engaged in one of their favorite sports: stealing parts of parked cars. Normally, nothing dramatic would have happened, as the police have not been present in that suburb for years. The problem came when one of the inhabitants, a female busybody, telephoned the police and reported the thieving spree taking place just opposite her building. The police were thus obliged to do something – which meant entering a city that, as noted, had been a no-go area for them.

Once the police arrived on the scene, the youths – who had been reigning over Clichy pretty unmolested for years – got really angry. A brief chase took place in the street, and two of the youths, who were not actually chased by the police, sought refuge in a cordoned-off area housing a power pylon. Both were electrocuted.

Once news of their deaths was out, Clichy was all up in arms. With cries of 'God is great,' bands of youths armed with whatever they could get hold of went on a rampage and forced the police to flee. The French authorities could not allow a band of youths to expel the police from French territory. So they hit back – sending in Special Forces, known as the CRS, with armored cars and tough rules of engagement.[5]

Within hours, the original cause of the incidents was forgotten and the issue jelled around a demand by the representatives of the rioters that the French police leave the 'occupied territories'. By midweek, the riots had spread to three of the provinces neighboring Paris, with a population of 5.5 million.

But who lives in the affected areas? In Clichy itself, more than 80 percent of the inhabitants are Muslim immigrants or their children, mostly from Arab and black Africa. In other affected towns, the Muslim immigrant community accounts for 30 percent to 60 percent of the population. But these are not the only figures that matter. Average unemployment in the affected areas is estimated at around 30 percent and, when it comes to young would-be workers, reaches 60 percent. In these suburban towns, built in the 1950s in imitation of the Soviet social housing[6] of the Stalinist era, people live in crammed conditions, sometimes several generations in a tiny apartment, and see 'real French life' only on television. The French used to flatter themselves for the success of their policy of assimilation, which was supposed to turn immigrants from any background into 'proper Frenchmen' within a generation at most. That policy worked as long as immigrants came to France in drips and drops and thus could merge into a much larger mainstream. Assimilation, however, cannot work when in most schools in the affected areas, fewer than 20 percent of the pupils are native

---

[5]**rules of engagement**   military regulations that set limits on how forces will initiate and continue action with other forces

[6]**Soviet social housing**   grey blocks of high-rise concrete apartments that were built in the Soviet Union during the earlier part of the 20th century

French speakers. France has also lost another powerful mechanism for assimilation: the obligatory military service abolished in the 1990s.

As the number of immigrants and their descendants increases in a particular locality, more and more of its native French inhabitants leave for 'calmer places', thus making assimilation still more difficult. In some areas, it is possible for an immigrant or his descendants to spend a whole life without ever encountering the need to speak French, let alone familiarize himself with any aspect of the famous French culture. The result is often alienation. And that, in turn, gives radical Islamists an opportunity to propagate[7] their message of religious and cultural apartheid.[8] Some are even calling for the areas where Muslims form a majority of the population to be reorganized on the basis of the 'millet' system of the Ottoman Empire: Each religious community (millet) would enjoy the right to organize its social, cultural and educational life in accordance with its religious beliefs. In parts of France, a de facto millet system is already in place. In these areas, all women are obliged to wear the standardized Islamist 'hijab' while most men grow their beards to the length prescribed by the sheiks. The radicals have managed to chase away French shopkeepers selling alcohol[8] and pork products[9], forced 'places of sin,' such as dancing halls, cinemas and theaters, to close down, and seized control of much of the local administration.

A reporter who spent last weekend in Clichy and its neighboring towns of Bondy, Aulnay-sous-Bois and Bobigny heard a single overarching message: The French authorities should keep out.

'All we demand is to be left alone,' said Mouloud Dahmani, one of the local 'emirs'[10] engaged in negotiations to persuade the French to withdraw the police and allow a committee of sheiks,[10]

---

[7]**propagate**   broadcast, advertise
[8]**apartheid**   separateness
[9]**alcohol/pork products**   these are forbidden in the Muslim diet
[10]**emirs/sheiks**   Arab chiefs

mostly from the Muslim Brotherhood, to negotiate an end to the hostilities.

President Jacques Chirac and Premier de Villepin are especially sore because they had believed that their opposition to the toppling of Saddam Hussein in 2003 would give France a heroic image in the Muslim community. That illusion has now been shattered – and the Chirac administration, already passing through a deepening political crisis, appears to be clueless about how to cope with what the Parisian daily *France Soir* has called a 'ticking time bomb'. It is now clear that a good portion of France's Muslims not only refuse to assimilate into 'the superior French culture', but firmly believe that Islam offers the highest forms of life to which all mankind should aspire.

So what is the solution? One solution, offered by Gilles Kepel, an adviser to Chirac on Islamic affairs, is the creation of 'a new Andalusia' in which Christians and Muslims would live side by side and cooperate to create a new cultural synthesis. The problem with Kepel's vision, however, is that it does not address the important issue of political power. Who will rule this new Andalusia: Muslims or the largely secularist Frenchmen? Suddenly, French politics has become worth watching again, even though for the wrong reasons.

Further reading

If you wish to learn more about the background to the French riots in 2005, you can visit some of the main news websites such as Times Online or Guardian Unlimited and enter a search term such as 'French riots 2005' or 'Paris riots 2005'.

Stuart: A Life Backwards

by Alexander Masters

Stuart: A Life Backwards is an award-winning book, which was turned into a BBC television drama in 2006. It tells the story of Stuart Shorter, a homeless alcoholic with a violent past, who strikes up an unlikely friendship with charity worker Alexander Masters who asks if he can write his life story. Stuart advises him to tell the story backwards, so that it is more mysterious – like a thriller; how did Stuart end up as he did? This extract describes some of the places designed to help people like Stuart, but also the problems the homeless and troubled face trying to escape from their way of life.

Show a tiny element of responsibility, don't assault anyone or openly take drugs, and the staff at Wintercomfort Day Centre will connect you to the outreach team, who will get you into a hostel, usually an English Churches Housing property. Willow Walk hostel for rough sleepers, or Willow Walk's big sister, 222 Victoria Road, are the ones. They have small private rooms with settled accommodation. At 222, there are seventy-four beds. A Dantesque[1] institution with an innocuous pale brick façade not far from where I live, I pass by it on my way to the local supermarket. Occasionally there are ambulances or a police car outside: somebody has overdosed, been beaten up, been beating someone else up or smashed the window of a nearby off-licence and come stumbling back with an armful of chilled beers. It is run by a friend of mine, a conscientious, highly intelligent, imaginative woman who, with her staff, performs something of a miracle to keep this place going every day.

There is a constant air of watchfulness in places like 222 (especially) and Willow Walk (to a much lesser extent). Long periods of quiet are followed by short tempests of violence in which it seems people are 'kicking off' on every wing and the

---

[1]**Dantesque**   like the work of the 13th/14th-century Italian poet: austere

housing officers rush from one incident to the next, clatter along the corridors with fingers on walkie-talkie buttons wondering if the full moon has snagged on the nearby traffic lights.[2]

This is why Stuart hates hostels. 'Because in them places you've got little kids trying to be bully boys and they see someone small and skinny like me, and with a limp, and to people like that I'm an easy target. So I have to deal with them in a severe way, if they take a liberty, to get the message, then I end up in nick again. Well, I can't condemn them because I used to be the same. But if the person killed me, I wouldn't like him to end up having to do even three years in prison. I wouldn't wish it on nobody.'

'You didn't mind the idea of getting three drunks from the pub to kill you, risking their imprisonment,' I remind him.

'Yeah – but they weren't homeless.'

Hostels are not right for most people. They become (as the pun goes) hostiles. Or, worse, a sense of contentment creeps up on the residents. After six months, outrageous incidents are no longer reasons for threatening staff with letters of complaint to the chief executive or promising to tip off the *Cambridge Evening News* – they are gossip. Street life is testimony to man's self-defeating powers of adaptation. The same thing applies in prison: people get used to the outrage of the new circumstances – they give up trying to fight back. John Brock, the former Wintercomfort manager that Stuart and I are campaigning for, is a good example. After a few months inside, he writes to his wife that prison has started to feel right. He likes it when the warden closes the cell door on him. He is beginning to feel that it is easier to be guilty.

Hostels, despite all their best efforts, encourage drug addiction and alcoholism. The main reason why Stuart demanded that the council give him a flat five miles outside of Cambridge was to get away from the city's drug and petty crime set. Putting a man trying to get off heroin and burglaries in a homeless

---

[2] **full moon . . . traffic lights**　there is a belief that some people are moved to violence or madness at the time of the full moon

hostel, no matter how dedicated the support staff, is like putting a paedophile in a kindergarten. Temptation is everywhere. The only place that has more drugs in it than a homeless centre is prison.

At 222, Stuart got beaten up and didn't squeal; got beaten up again and still kept his mouth shut; got beaten up a third time, head-butted one of the bullies, 'split all his eye open', had a knife fight with another and had to leave.

He wouldn't go in Jimmy's, either, in the basement of the Zion Baptist Church on the other side of town. Technically, Jimmy's is a 'shelter' rather than a 'hostel': people do not have rooms there, just the possibility of a bed in a dormitory, which must be arranged night by night. No alcohol, body searches at the door and no sin bins in which to deposit your needles safely.

'There's some nice people who go down Jimmy's, but you get a lot of the mentally ill and the drunks down there. And they chuck you out the door at nine o'clock in the morning. They get a good whack of money for you staying there but they put you out on the street at nine o'clock in the morning till half seven at night.'

Jimmy's, named after a charismatic dosser, another of the homeless now-dead, is something of a throwback to George Orwell flophouses,[3] though a good example of one. It can be a stabilising place for people who would otherwise spend all night on the beer and brown. But it's useless for someone who likes privacy, or is easily bullied, or has a persecution complex,[4] or likes to sleep in a dress, or snores so loudly that the other residents gang up and stuff a sock in his mouth.

Whatever service you provide, no matter how welcoming, tolerant, well staffed and decorated with pretty pot plants, there will always be homeless people it doesn't suit.

---

[3]**George Orwell flophouses**   a reference to the author George Orwell's personal account of living on the streets in London and Paris in the early 20th century: *Down and Out in Paris and London*

[4]**persecution complex**   personal belief that everyone in the world is hostile

'Because that's the point of them, in't it?' explains Stuart. 'The homeless are what's left over after all the usual things what keep people straight and narrow – yes sir, no sir, three bags full sir – like family, career, the army, have been taken out.'

For a year while writing this book I worked at the Willow Walk hostel, the best hostel in the city: twenty-two beds, single rooms, twenty-four-hour staff sitting in an office by the door. Rent: £279 a week per person. (The homeless don't pay that, of course. They pay around £6.50. The rest comes through housing benefit, from you and me.) It is run by Ruth's husband, a kind, relaxed and thoughtful man.

The residents at Willow Walk are in general pleasant, although some individuals have their moments. (The list of people banned from the premises, for example, includes one with six convictions for attempted murder and another for trying to kill a hostel worker.) They are essentially a cautious, edgy crowd who, when they 'lose it', are raging against their own losses more than against anyone else. Some of them have experienced things that would make you throw up if you knew the details, but they don't become serial killers, arsonists, letter bombers. They doubt, they grizzle, they stamp about their little cubicle rooms, they suspect everything is their fault (or they think nothing is their fault and therefore think they have no control over their existence), they cut themselves, they watch the days and months slip by, they get smashed out of their skulls. Some are hilarious, some are very talented, many are kindly, many are boring, a few were once rich, a good number are to some degree insane. Some are so apologetic it is unsettling. They might have been a bit rude to you the day before, called you a 'twat' (frequently with some justice) or just stumbled about for a while, being merry and foolish. But they apologise at the soonest sober opportunity, even when the person listening to these sorries hasn't the foggiest idea what they're on about any longer. It is impossible to be precise in characterising the people who live in such places. In my own estimate, about a quarter of them you could pass on the street and not have the faintest reason to think they are anything other than successful (the best-dressed man in Cambridge at the moment is a man living in Jimmy's). But alongside these are the usual stereotype figures so beloved by people who write about low-life: the crackheads, the dope fiends, the Irish drunks, the nonces, the whores (but don't read that word in a Raymond Chandler voice – think instead of pallid girls with fungal infections, and grandmothers who'll let you feel their varicose veins in return for a mouthful of half-digested beer), the burglars, the shoplifters, the ambitionless, the self-disgusted, the weak of will and, very rarely, the just plain poor.

The final step on the ladder of opportunity – after Wintercomfort, Jimmy's, 222 Victoria Road, the young persons' project in Haverhill, Willow Walk, Emmaus,[5] temporary shared housing with organisations such as the Cyrenians – is to be put into a bedsit or flat of your own.

If this rehabilitation process works well, you can be off the streets, in accommodation of your own and looking for a new job within half a year, though even that is not quick enough. On average, it takes nine years for a person, after the event that has unsettled them (abuse, bankruptcy, marriage break-up, etc.), to become homeless. It then takes four weeks to become 'entrenched', i.e. to settle into street life and begin to adapt irrevocably.*

But the ladder hardly ever works well – at least, not with 'chaotic' rough sleepers. Stuart's sort do not live under the stars and endure piles and hypothermia simply because they've run out of luck and 'self-esteem'. Therefore, it's not just a matter of providing encouragement, vocational training and money to put them back on their feet. To them, every day is a hum of casual outrages. In the worst cases such a person is hardly human at all, but like the shell of a man walking around crammed with minced ego. It is as though some piece of their

---

[5]**Emmaus**   a hostel for men who make a living by recycling household goods
*Statistics from Shelter.

soul is missing. The way he is and the manner in which he lives are symptoms of a mental disruption – maybe even a full-blown incurable illness – and it is as good to tell him to apply for one of the fifty warehouse packing jobs advertised in the employ-ment office as it is to tell a man with half a leg to drop his crutches and run home.

'See, the homeless culture is a weird culture,' explains Stuart. 'One minute they're all fighting against each other, but then there's days we all stick together through thick and thin, all different little groups. Like, once, I sat there begging with a fellow, and he just jumped up and started kicking me in the face. He don't know why neither.'

At one point, in an effort to get away from this mayhem hostel and street life, Stuart bought a caravan for £25 and had it towed down to the river, but something came a cropper there too. Other people took it over. He let the wrong friends sleep on the floor. They set light to it. It exploded.

Another time, Stuart got into an argument with Frank the Tank, and Frank the Tank walloped him in the park behind the bus shelter. Result: bus shelter out of bounds.

'Even if you get a job, you're caught in a Catch-22, because the only time you can get work is if you're living at one of the hostels, because no one gives you work if you haven't got an address. But if you get a job when you're staying there, the staff immediately raise the rent. They got to, because them rooms cost £200–300 a week and benefits won't pay the full whack any more if you got a job, will they? It might go up to £60–70 a week, overnight, from the first day you get work! Frightening to someone who was paying a fiver a week the day before. But this is the stupid bit: legal jobs don't pay except in arrears. Two weeks, a month in arrears, that's when you get the first pay cheque. How can you pay the new ridiculous rent them first four weeks? It isn't possible. Where's the money going to come from? Get a job and what happens? Get kicked out of your accommodation for non-payment of rent.'

I do know about this. I have myself advised homeless people not to get work, especially if they have just arrived on the streets (the benefits situation improves slightly if you've been down and out for six months, although by that time the sense of community with the homeless, and sense of homelessness not being that bad really, has set in) because if they do they will lose their hostel accommodation, and hence their job, too, for exactly the reason Stuart describes.

In short, at every step up the ladder, the chaotic homeless person will stumble. He throws a tantrum, loses his nerve, drinks himself to the brink of oblivion, ends up in the police cells and three weeks later has to be restarted on the bottom rung by people who grow increasingly tired of seeing his mottled face.

This is why Stuart, sicker than most, within a few weeks of leaving Smudger's flat, fell off the ladder and sank like a stone.

Much of what happened over the next four months before the outreach team found him is, even to himself, a blank.

Further reading

On the surface, *Stuart* is part of the series of texts sometimes referred to as 'Misery Memoirs', but partly because it is not an autobiography, and because of the fact it is written 'backwards' from the present to the past, it is rather different. If the more conventional structure is easier for you to read, try *Street Kid: One child's desperate fight for survival* by Judy Westwater (Harper Element, 2006). This is very hard-hitting, however.

The Centre of the Universe

by Paul Durcan

In this poem, Paul Durcan describes a series of phone calls, some of which sound absurd, others more realistic, to which the poet responds in different ways. But what happens when the poet is alone and needs help himself?

i   Pushing my trolley about in the supermarket,
    I am the centre of the universe;
    Up and down the aisles of beans and juices,
    I am the centre of the universe;
    It does not matter that I live alone;
    It does not matter that I am a jilted lover;
    It does not matter that I am a misfit in my job;
    I am the centre of the universe.

    But I'm always here, if you want me –
    For I am the centre of the universe.

ii I enjoy being the centre of the universe.
    It is not easy being the centre of the universe
    But I enjoy it.
    I take pleasure in,
    I delight in,
    Being the centre of the universe.
    At six o'clock a.m. this morning I had a phone call;
    It was from a friend, a man in Los Angeles:
    'Paul, I don't know what time it is in Dublin
    But I simply had to call you:
    I cannot stand LA so I thought I'd call you.'
    I calmed him down as best I could.

    I'm always here, if you want me –
    For I am the centre of the universe.

iii I had barely put the phone down when it rang again,
This time from a friend in São Paulo in Brazil:
'Paul – do you know what is the population of São Paulo?
I will tell you: it is twelve million skulls.
Twelve million pairs of feet in the one footbath.
Twelve million pairs of eyes in the one fishbowl.
It is unspeakable, I tell you, unspeakable.'
I calmed him down.

I'm always here, if you want me –
For I am the centre of the universe.

iv But then when the phone rang a third time and it was not
    yet 6.30 a.m.,
The petals of my own hysteria began to wake up and unfurl.
This time it was a woman I know in New York City:
'Paul – New York City is a Cage',
And she began to cry a little bit over the phone,

To sob over the phone,
And from five thousand miles away I mopped up her tears.
I dabbed each tear from her cheek
With just a word or two or three from my calm voice.

I'm always here, if you want me –
For I am the centre of the universe.

v   But now tonight it is myself;
Sitting at my aluminium double-glazed window in
    Dublin city;
Crying just a little bit into my black tee shirt.
If only there was just one human being out there
With whom I could make a home? Share a home?
Just one creature out there in the night –
Is there not just one creature out there in the night?
In Helsinki, perhaps? Or in Reykjavik?
Or in Chapelizod? Or in Malahide?
So you see, I have to calm myself down also
If I am to remain the centre of the universe;
It's by no means an exclusively self-centred automatic thing
Being the centre of the universe.

I'm always here, if you want me –
For I am the centre of the universe.

Further reading

This poem could be described as being intensely personal, and if you
would like to read more of Paul's work, look up his entry on Wikepedia
for a list of his poetry collections, such as *Daddy, Daddy* (1990) and *The
Berlin Wall Café* (1985).

Activities

Harassment

Before you read

1 What is the meaning of 'harassment'? Write your own definition and compare it with that of a partner. If you are not sure, you may need to look it up using a thesaurus or dictionary.

2 Think about any dialect words you know. Copy the table below and add dialect words and their Standard English equivalents.

Dialect word or phrase	Standard English version or meaning
bairn	baby/child

What's it about?

3 With a partner, take turns to read the poem aloud, helping each other with any pronunciations you might find difficult. Then, discuss together:

- What dialect and accent do you think are used in the poem?
- What is the basic story the poem tells? (Try to sum it up as simply as possible.)

4 What makes this a poem? Why is it in verses, for example? With the same partner, jot down an explanatory line for each verse, as follows:

Verse 1: **The poet describes returning from work and being stopped by police.**

Now discuss whether there are any other examples of poetic features, for example rhyme, rhythm, pattern of lines, and so on. If there are, what do these add?

Thinking about the text

5 Write a response to this essay title:

'This poem is about much more than a man being wrongly accused of planning a robbery – do you agree?'

Consider the poet's anger, and the wider statements he makes about the situation for black people.

Little Soldier

Before you read

1   Although the country from which Kaninda comes is a fictional one, it bears many similarities to Rwanda. What do you know about the conflict in Rwanda in the early to mid 1990s? Research what happened, and find out:

-   where Rwanda is
-   who the rival groups/tribes were
-   how it started, and how peace was agreed.

What's it about?

2   Discuss with a partner what impressions we get of Laura and Kaninda from Scene 1, and Scene 2 up to the point where Sergeant Matu appears. In particular, consider:

-   what each character appears to want (their motivation)
-   the ways they react to others.

Then move into a group and share your findings with the others.

3   How does the writer build up suspense when Kaninda finally does the run? Take each of these points and write one sentence, explaining what the writer does, and referring to a relevant quotation.

-   Length of lines of speech
-   Use of punctuation
-   Use of stage directions (in brackets, mostly)
-   Use of repetition

4   In small groups, prepare a rehearsed reading of the extract. Once you have been given your character, consider how you can use your voice:

-   for expression (to show emotion, excitement, fear etc.)
-   to help the flow/pace (speak quickly, pause, interrupt?)
-   for accent/dialect (there are several clues to pronunciation in the script).

Thinking about the text

5   Write a short story called 'Child Soldier' in which you are a pupil at school who is told to look after a new boy/girl who has come from a war zone overseas. Describe your first day with him/her and how they react to everyday life in the UK.

Ex-gang Member Opens LA Airwaves to Street Voices

Before you read

1 What skills do you think you need in order to be a good radio talk-show host? Consider any shows or hosts you have listened to, and which you thought were particularly good. List the skills needed, and then compare what you have written with a partner's list.

What's it about?

2 The article consists of three main elements: the talk-show host Taylor, his life and views; the people who call in, and their stories; and wider information about the state of gangs, police etc. in LA. Work in groups of three and make brief notes, taking one area each, writing down what you find out. Then, feed back your information within your group. Agree what you think the *purpose* of the article is.

3 The writer makes a lot of reference to specialist or informal terms related to radio, for example:

'chunks of dead air'
'mainstream commercial radio'
'dense media market'
'ad dollars'
'market-tested playlists'
'golden-throated disc jockeys'.

On your own, scan the text to find each of these phrases, and then jot down what you think each means (in its context).

Thinking about the text

4 The article suggests that the show is a bit of an experiment. In groups discuss:
  • why such a show might be controversial
  • whether you think the show is a good idea
  • who the target audience is (think carefully – it may be wider than you think!).

5 Make a list of five questions you might ask Bo Taylor, then role-play an interview with a partner (one of you playing Bo).

6 The article begins with a young man called Curtis, who lives in a gang area. Write a letter to him offering advice about his situation. Be realistic, and take account of the problems he faces.

Why Paris is Burning

Before you read

1 What would it be like to be caught up in night-time riots in a city? How would you feel if you were a member of the police sent to calm things down, or make arrests? Or, how would you feel if you were one of the rioters, convinced that the police were the cause of the problems?

What's it about?

2 Many news reports start by telling us the key facts – the *who*, *what*, *where*, *when* and *why* of a situation. With a partner, re-read the first paragraph and make notes on each of these points. Then, discuss:
   - How is this different from most conventional news reports?
   - How does the title imply that this is not so much a news report as an analytical article?

3 How does the writer use questions to structure the article as a whole? Does the article end by answering all the questions? Share your thoughts among a group.

4 There is quite a lot of difficult vocabulary and references in the text. Working in a group, divide up the text and research words or phrases you don't understand, first having tried to work out their meanings in context.

Thinking about the text

5 In a group, discuss what you think the view of the writer is – is he sympathetic to the immigrant communities, the French government – or neither?

6 Imagine you are a police officer who was sent to the area. You now have to write an official report for your boss, describing what happened. It must be written in factual, formal language. For example: We arrived at Clichy-sous-Bois at approximately 9 pm to apprehend the youths involved in the theft of vehicle parts. On arrival, we noted a group who were . . .

Stuart: A Life Backwards

Before you read

1   Have you ever visited, or seen, shelters or hostels for the homeless? Draw a quick sketch of one, or a plan of its layout. Label the facilities on offer. Keep your sketch/plan to hand and see how close your image is to the reality described by Alexander Masters.

What's it about?

2   Re-read from the beginning of the text to '. . . a knife fight with another and had to leave'. What view is given of the hostel at 222 Victoria Road by:
*   the writer
*   Stuart?

Share your thoughts in a group and decide whether the view/s is or are positive or negative and why.

3   What view of Stuart do you get from this extract? Write your own character description of him based on what he says about himself, and his life, and also based on what the writer tells us about him. Choose your adjectives or nouns carefully and support your views with examples from the text.

Thinking about the text

4   The writer talks about the 'ladder of opportunity' which the homeless have to climb, but at the end of the text Stuart describes the 'Catch-22' situation of what happens if the homeless finally do get a job. Discuss in a group:
*   What do you think 'Catch-22' situation means here?
*   Do you think the writer was right to advise homeless people 'not to get work'?

5   What do you think are the qualities needed in someone to manage a homeless centre or shelter? Write an advert for a manager for such a place based on what you have read in this extract.

The Centre of the Universe

Before you read

1 Bring in a photo, or draw a basic sketch, of yourself, and place it in the middle of a large piece of paper. Then add words or images on the paper that represent your 'universe' – what's around you in the room, names of friends, places you know or go to, and so on.

What's it about?

2 Each verse of the poem deals with a slightly different situation for the poet, and his feelings about his life. Copy the following table and complete it with a partner:

Verse	Time and place	Outside world	Information about poet
1	Time: unknown Place: supermarket	Supermarket; no people mentioned	'alone', 'jilted lover', 'misfit'
2		Friend in Los Angeles on phone	
3			

3 Why is this a poem? Make notes about the poetic techniques used here, for example:
   - repetition of words, phrases or lines
   - other patterns or rhythms
   - speaking directly to the reader.

Thinking about the text

4 What impression do we get of the poet and the sort of person he is? Write a short character study of him, including evidence in the form of quotations or examples from the poem.

5 Write a poem called 'Lonely People' made up of five verses.
   a In each verse, describe a person in a different part of the world (for example, a child soldier in Africa; a homeless tramp in Manchester).
   b Include a repeated refrain after each verse, such as 'All the lonely people / All the lonely people, where do they all come from?'

Compare and contrast

1   There are two poems in this section – 'Harassment' and 'The Centre of the Universe'. Write a comparison of them, in which you consider: the stories they tell, the feelings of the poets, and the language and structures they use to convey their ideas.

2   To what extent is 'race' or 'ethnic background' an important theme or issue in any of these extracts? Discuss this question in groups and refer carefully to examples from the texts.

3   Which of these texts do you think presents the most positive or hopeful view of people who feel they are outsiders? Create a list of the texts, with the most positive at the top, and then compare your list with a partner's. Do you agree/disagree? Justify your choices.

4   The section presents different ways in which outsiders' voices are heard by the audience or reader, for example through a performed play, a radio show, a newspaper report, a book etc. Which do you think is the best way of giving these people a voice? (Think carefully about the advantages/disadvantages of, say, something in print as opposed to a radio show.)

5   Finally, which of these texts made the greatest impression on you? Write a short essay explaining your choice.

Notes on authors

George Alagiah (1955–) is a BBC news presenter, journalist and writer. Originally from Sri Lanka, he lived briefly in Ghana before coming to the UK where he attended school in Hampshire. He joined the BBC in 1989 after a spell working for magazines, and worked as a foreign correspondent around the world before becoming the main news presenter. He was awarded an OBE in 2008.

Bernard Ashley (1935–) is a picture-book writer, playwright and novelist who lives in London and writes predominantly for teenagers and young people. His stories, such as *The Trouble with Donovan Croft* (1974) and *Running Scared* (1986), have exciting plots with emotional power and have been shortlisted for many awards such as the Carnegie and Guardian Young Fiction prize. He has also written for television, adapting his own novel *Dodgem* (1982) into a series which won the Royal Television Society award for Best Children's Entertainment.

Lutaa Badamkhand (1964–) is a Mongolian journalist who has worked for a number of national and international newspapers and news agencies.

William Blake (1757–1827) was a poet and painter who went unrecognised during his own lifetime. Rejecting conventional religious views he invented his own mythology, and composed powerful collections of poems such as *Songs of Innocence* (1789) and *Songs of Experience* (1794). His etchings and paintings often accompanied his work and are almost as famous as the words he wrote. He is perhaps best known today for writing the words to the hymn 'Jerusalem'.

Bill Bryson (1951–) is an American journalist and humorist who has lived in both the UK and the USA. Best known for his humorous travel books such as *The Lost Continent* (1989), *Neither Here nor There* (1991) and *Notes from a Small Island* (1995), Bryson is also an accomplished writer about language, as his books *Mother Tongue* (1990) and *Made in America* (1994) demonstrate. He has more recently turned his hand to popular science with *A Short History of Nearly Everything* (2003). He was awarded an OBE in 2006.

Rory Carroll is a foreign correspondent who works for *The Guardian*. He worked in Italy and South Africa before becoming one of the paper's correspondents in Baghdad, where he was briefly abducted in 2005 before being released.

Tony Connor (1930–) is a poet and playwright, and is a Fellow of the Royal Society of Literature. He was Professor of English at a university in Connecticut, USA until his retirement in 1999.

Charles Dickens (1812–70) was an English novelist and social campaigner, who experienced poverty before making his name with a series of powerful novels, many of which are set in London. His most famous include *A Christmas Carol, Oliver Twist, Bleak House* and *David Copperfield*. He began his writing as a journalist, but quickly made his name with his novels which were serialised in magazines of the time. His novels feature memorable characters and settings, with lots of different plots and stories connecting together. Many of his works have been serialised for television, turned into films – and, of course, musicals and stage-plays.

Paul Durcan (1944–) is a poet from Dublin whose works have won awards such as The Whitbread Prize for his collection *Daddy, Daddy* (1990). His work is lyrical, and can be surreal but also deals with day-to-day concerns and the 'big issues' to do with Irish history and society.

Zulfikar Ghose (1935–) is a poet and writer of fiction and non-fiction. Originally born in a part of India that became Pakistan, he moved to the UK and then settled in America where he lectures at the University of Texas. He has written about a wide range of subjects, including the immigrant experience, but has also written critical works on Shakespeare and others.

Andrew Glazer is a journalist and reporter who writes on a wide range of issues for Associated Press.

Sally Grindley (1953–) is an award-winning picture-book writer and children's novelist. *Spilled Water* won several prizes including the Smarties Prize Gold Award in 2004. Her novel *Broken Glass* (2008) is about two runaways in an Indian city, whilst *Torn Pages* (2009) deals with the effects of AIDS in Sierra Leone.

Lynsey Hanley (1976–) writes for a range of magazines and newspapers such as the *Observer,* the *Guardian* and *New Statesman. Estates* is her first book.

Thomas Hardy (1840–1928) was a novelist and poet who wrote mostly about the life and situations of people in the south-west of England – specifically his own home county of Dorset. His most famous works are his novels, such as *Far from the Madding Crowd* (1874), *The Mayor of Casterbridge* (1886) and the controversial *Tess of the d'Urbervilles* (1891) which was initially refused publication. These often dealt with the conflict between countryside and town, and people's struggle to better their lives. In his later years he began to write poetry and published his first collection, *Wessex Poems*, in 1898.

Meg Harper (1960–) is a children's author who writes for younger children and teenagers. Her works include the *My Mum and . . .* series and *Fur* (Usborne, 2006). She also runs drama workshops and gives talks in schools about being a writer.

Robert Harris (1957–) was once a reporter for the BBC, political editor for *The Observer* and a writer for *The Sunday Times* and other papers, before turning his hand to novels to become one of the best-selling writers of today. His first novel was *Fatherland* in 1992, and he subsequently wrote *Enigma* (1995), *Archangel* (1998) and, following *Pompeii* (2003) and *Imperium* (2006), turned his attention to modern times with a book about a ghost-writer called *The Ghost.*

S. E. Hinton (1948–) wrote *The Outsiders* while still a teenager living in Tulsa, Oklahoma, and has gone on to write other novels about similar characters and situations, such as *That Was Then, This Is Now* (1971) and *Rumble Fish* (1975). All three novels have been made into films, and have helped launch the careers of actors such as Matt Dillon.

Khaled Hosseini (1965–) was born and raised in Afghanistan, but because of violent civil war eventually moved to Paris, and then on to the USA. He is the author of two best-selling novels – *The Kite Runner* (2003) which was made into a film in 2007, and *A Thousand Splendid Suns* (2007). His writing deals with the plight of different groups and factions trying to survive in a war-torn country.

Brian Keenan (1951–) became famous when he was kidnapped in Beirut in 1986, spending four years in captivity until his release in 1990. At the time of his capture he was teaching at the American University but after his release he concentrated on writing the account of his ordeal, *An Evil Cradling* (1992), and has since published other works including travel books such as *Four Quarters of Light: An Alaskan Journey* (2005).

D. H. Lawrence (1885–1930) is best-known as a short-story writer, novelist and poet, who wrote frankly about relationships, family life and town and countryside. His style is often poetic in its power. His most famous works include *Sons and Lovers* (1913), *The Rainbow* (1915) and *Women in Love* (1920) but it is his novel *Lady Chatterley's Lover* which caused particular controversy. Featuring the love affair between an aristocrat and her gamekeeper, it was banned for 30 years until a famous court case in 1960 allowed Penguin to publish it.

Graham Marks (1949–) has written articles for magazines, scripts for radio and television, and run an advertising agency as well as writing teenage fiction. His novels include *Snatched* (2006), *Radio Radio* (2003) and *Omega Place* (2007), which is about a boy who runs away from home to join a secretive group who object to all the surveillance devices in the UK and seek to destroy them.

Alexander Masters was born in New York but grew up in Devon before studying at Cambridge and then becoming a charity worker, where he met Stuart, the subject of his first book – *Stuart: A Life Lived Backwards* (2005) – which won the Guardian First Book Award.

Jon McGregor (1976–) is a British novelist who has written *If Nobody Speaks of Remarkable Things* (nominated for the 2002 Booker Prize), and *So Many Ways to Begin* (2006).

Beverley Naidoo (1943–) is an award-winning children's author who won the Carnegie Medal in 2000 for her novel *The Other Side of Truth*. She grew up in South Africa and was arrested at one point for her opposition to the apartheid movement. In 1965 she moved to Britain and it was there that she wrote most of her novels, including *Journey to Jo'burg* (1986) which was banned by the South African apartheid government of the time.

V. S. Naipaul (1932–), winner of the Nobel Prize for Literature in 2001, was born in Trinidad, but of Indian origin, thus giving his books a genuinely multicultural flavour. His most famous works are the novels *A House for Mr Biswas* (1961), *In a Free State* (1971) and *A Bend in the River* (1979) but he has also written a wide range of non-fiction, much of it about India. He was knighted in 1990.

Andrew O'Hagan (1968–) is an award-winning Scottish writer and novelist. His book *The Missing* was published in 1995 and later filmed as a documentary by Channel 4. His novels include *Our Fathers* (1999) and *Be Near Me* (2006), both nominated for the Booker Prize.

Mark Powell grew up in Loughton, Essex, and the East End of London. At 19, fascinated by hip-hop culture, he went to New York to seek excitement, but he discovered life on the streets was hard, living with a gang who scraped money together by begging and stealing. His urge to write brought him back to the UK where he studied for a novel-writing MA at Manchester University. *Box* is his second novel.

Raekha Prasad is a journalist who writes for the *Guardian* and *The Times*. She is well-known for her articles highlighting India's widespread poverty and corruption.

Bali Rai (1971–) is a novelist who has written on a range of topics for young people. His *Devana High* stories deal with a school and its students, whilst many of his other novels, such as *The Whisper* and *The Crew* (2003), have an urban, multi-ethnic setting with hard-hitting storylines.

Adam Sage is a journalist who writes for various papers and magazines such as *The Times* and *New Statesman*.

Amir Taheri (1942–) is an Iranian-born journalist and author based in Europe. His writings focus on Middle East affairs and topics related to Islamist terrorism. As well as his written work he has also interviewed world leaders, including several American presidents, and has produced a number of television documentaries.

Frederick Williams (1965–), now known as 'Omara', is a poet and performer. Originally from Jamaica, he has lived in the UK for over

35 years, but continues to write and perform in Jamaican dialect. He often writes about the day-to-day experiences of black people. His collections include *Me Memba Wen* and *Leggo de Pen*.

Jeanette Winterson (1959–) is a novelist who is most famous for her debut work *Oranges Are Not The Only Fruit* (1985), which won The Whitbread Prize and was made into an acclaimed television drama in 1990. *Tanglewreck* is her first novel for children.

William Wordsworth (1770–1850) was born and brought up in the Lake District in northern England, and is best known for his poetry celebrating nature and the power of the imagination. One of the poets most associated with the Romantic movement in literature, his most famous single poem is probably *Daffodils* ('I wandered lonely as a cloud . . .'). He was made Poet Laureate in 1843.

Acknowledgements

The volume editor and publishers acknowledge the following sources of copyright material and are grateful for the permissions granted. While every effort has been made, it has not always been possible to identify the sources of all the material used, or to trace all copyright holders. If any omissions are brought to our notice, we will be happy to include the appropriate acknowledgement on reprinting.

p. 2 from *Tokyo* by Graham Marks, published by Bloomsbury; p. 8 from *India: A Million Mutinies Now* by V. S. Naipaul, © V. S. Naipaul; p. 12 from *Pompeii* by Robert Harris, published by Hutchinson, reprinted by permission of The Random House Group Ltd; p. 19 from *The Lost Continent* by Bill Bryson, published by Black Sawn, reprinted by permission of The Random House Group Ltd, copyright © Bill Bryson 1989, reprinted by permission of Doubleday Canada; p. 38 from *Spilled Water* by Sally Grindley, published by Bloomsbury; p. 42 from *No Turning Back* by Beverley Naidoo (Viking, 1995), copyright © Beverley Naidoo, 1995, reproduced by permission of Penguin Books Ltd; p. 50 from *Estates: An Intimate History* by Lynsey Hanley, published by Granta Books, reproduced by permission of United Agents on behalf of the author; p. 55 from *A Home From Home: From Immigrant Boy to English Man* by George Alagiah, published by Little, Brown, © George Alagiah 2006; p. 63 'This Landscape, These People' from *The Loss of India* by Zulfikar Ghose, copyright © 1964 Zulfikar Ghose, is reproduced by permission of Sheil Land Associates Ltd; p. 67 'Entering the City' is taken from *Things Unsaid: New and Selected Poems 1960–2005* by Tony Connor, published by Anvil Press Poetry in 2006; p. 69 'A Journey Back to My Hostage Hell' by Brian Keenan, *The Sunday Times*, 23 March 2008; p. 87 'The Railway Children' by Raekha Prasad, copyright Guardian News & Media Ltd 2007; p. 92 'São Paulo – City of the Future' by Rory Carroll, copyright Guardian News & Media Ltd 2008; p. 98 *The Missing* by Andrew O'Hagan, published by Pan Macmillan, London, copyright © Andrew O'Hagan 2004, by permission of A P Watt on behalf of Andrew O'Hagan; p. 104 'The Lost Sewer Children' by Lutaa Badamkhand, © *The Independent*, 16 December 2003; p. 117 *If Nobody Speaks of Remarkable Things* by Jon McGregor, published by Bloomsbury; p. 133 from *Tanglewreck* by Jeanette Winterson, published by Bloomsbury; p. 138 from *Piper* by Meg Harper, by permission of

Usborne Publishing, 83–85 Saffron Hill, London EC1N 8RT, UK (www.usborne.com), copyright © 2007, Usborne Publishing Ltd; p. 142 'The Well-dressed Girl Gangs of Paris' by Adam Sage, *The Times*, 23 February 2008; p. 145 from *The Whisper* by Bali Rai, published by Corgi, reprinted by permission of The Random House Group Ltd; p. 149 *The Outsiders* by S. E. Hinton (Victor Gollancz, 1970), copyright © S. E. Hinton, 1967, reproduced by permission of Penguin Books Ltd, copyright © 1967 by S.E. Hinton, copyright renewed 1995, reprinted by permission of Curtis Brown Ltd, used by permission of www.penguin.com; p. 161 from *Box* by Mark Powell published by Weidenfeld and Nicolson, an imprint of The Orion Publishing Group, London, copyright © 2003 Mark Powell, reproduced with permission of Curtis Brown Group Ltd, London, on behalf of Mark Powell; p. 168 from *The Kite Runner* by Khaled Hosseini, published by Bloomsbury, extracted from *The Kite Runner* by Khaled Hosseini, copyright © Khaled Hosseini 2003, reprinted by permission of Doubleday Canada; p. 187 'Harassment' by Frederick Williams; p. 190 from *The Play of Little Soldier* by Bernard Ashley, reprinted by permission of Pearson Education; p. 198 'Ex-gang member opens LA airwaves to street voices' by Andrew Glazer, *The Associated Press*, March 25, 2007, used by permission of The Associated Press, copyright © 2008, all rights reserved; p. 202 'Why Paris is burning' by Amir Taheri, used by permission of the author; p. 207 *Stuart: A Life Backwards* by Alexander Masters, reprinted by permission of HarperCollins Publishers Ltd, copyright © 2005 Alexander Masters, reproduced by permission of the author c/o Rogers, Coleridge & White Ltd (20 Powis Mews, London W11 1JN); p. 214 'The Centre of the Universe' by Paul Durcan, copyright © Paul Durcan, reproduced by permission of the author c/o Rogers, Coleridge & White Ltd (20 Powis Mews, London W11 1JN).

The publishers would like to thank the following for permission to reproduce photographs: p. 3 Peter Schneiter / Alamy; p. 27 Mary Evans Picture Library; p. 51 Edward Moss / Alamy; p. 64 ersoy emin / Alamy; p. 85 Peter Treanor / Alamy; p. 88 Atul Loke / Panos Pictures; p. 143 © Jerome Sessini / Corbis; p. 150 Everett Collection / Rex Features; p. 188 David Hoffman Photo Library / Alamy; p. 203 Sipa Press / Rex Features.